# Blind Trust

## ...A Child's Legacy

*To hope and healing —*
*Karen Austin*

### by
### Karen Austin

Snowbird Books, Inc.
Post Office Box 22
Woodstock, GA 30188-0022

Austin, Karen
Blind Trust: A Child's Legacy

Copyright 1999

*Disclaimer:* The majority of names have been changed and some of the characters fictionalized. Any resemblance to these fictitious names, living or dead, is purely coincidental and unintentional. In addition, some identifying details that do not affect the message of the book have intentionally been altered. There may be some shifting in time, places, and characters and other liberties taken with the actual events described herein. Every effort has been taken to maintain the privacy of others without sacrificing the integrity of this book. I am grateful to those dear friends and family members who requested I use their real names as a tribute to our relationship.

**Library of Congress Cataloging-in-Publication Data**

Library of Congress Catalog Card Number 98-90422
ISBN  0-9665191-0-8      (trade paper)


Printed in the United States of America by
Morris Publishing * 3212 East Highway 30 * Kearney, NE  68847

Published by: Snowbird Books, Inc.
              Post Office Box 22
              Woodstock , GA 30188-0022

This book is dedicated
to victims of abuse everywhere who struggle
through the battles without understanding the war.

And to my daughters who understand firsthand that
"the sins of the fathers are visited upon the children
even unto the third and fourth generations".

# Acknowledgments

A special thank you to Dr. Robert Hatcher who restored my faith in doctors and who helped tremendously in the production and publication of this book.

I am grateful to Dr. Shannon Dammann who took the time to advise me on perfecting the manuscript and to Sandra Wood and Dr. Jill Breland at the Georgia Council on Child Abuse for the fine work they do.

To my best friend, Carolyn, for her unfailing patience and encouragement during the years it has taken to get this book into print; there are no words that will do justice to a friendship as true as ours.

And to my second mother, Mrs. Becky Jones, whose gentle spirit and steadfast love make her one of the great unsung heroines of this world. Your efforts have not been in vain nor your influence gone unnoticed.

# FOREWORD

"Blind trust" is one of those inherent gifts that all babies bring with them into the world. Innocence, trust, faith - faith in the goodness of the world, in human beings and in that spiritual realm which is greater than us all. These are the rights of every child. But some children are tragically and brutally robbed of these rights even in the earliest moments of life. Their trust betrayed, their innocence stolen, and their faith shattered by the harsh realities of child abuse. Yet, even in the face of such great suffering, the human spirit strives to survive and thrive.

Karen Austin's book has captured the essence of a true journey of survival of the human spirit. With great courage and compassion she puts forth her heart and soul in the telling of her story; her nightmare, and her healing from the deep physical and spiritual wounding inflicted upon her throughout a terribly abusive childhood. She reveals how a young girl can find peace in fleeting moments of love, kindness, and nurturance in an otherwise dark and frightening world of abuse. She takes the reader along on her quest for spiritual understanding through her doubt and rediscovery of faith in goodness. She generously shares with anyone who chooses to listen the story of how she found her way to a healing path.

This book will certainly be a tremendous inspiration and resource to survivors of child abuse as well as to family members, partners, friends, and therapists who witness and share in their struggle.

Shannon M. Dammann, Psy.D.
Clinical Psychologist
Former Survivor Support Program Specialist
Georgia Council on Child Abuse

# PREFACE

*Blind Trust: A Child's Legacy* is a testimony to the indomitable human spirit, which we all have in common. There is nothing extraordinary about me, and therein lies the beauty of this message. It is the story of so many, many ordinary people and the ties that bind us. It is not the abuse itself, but rather the desire to rise above it, that draws us together. *Blind Trust: A Child's Legacy* is about coming of age in the deep South, about falling down and getting up again, about learning to cope, and about finding life worth living, after all.

You will find no pious, simple answers within these pages, because there are no pious, simple answers. What you will find is an honest look at a little girl's struggle to survive physically, emotionally, and spiritually in the all-too-common world of child abuse. For those who are unable to speak and for those who have been silenced forever, I offer my story on their behalf.

A word to those just embarking on the road to recovery: You may find some of the material in this book to be frightening or disturbing as it speaks to different stages of healing. Please know that this is a story of comfort and understanding, and you will be encouraged by the overall message. I hope you are in the process of surrounding yourself with people who value you and will give you the support you need. A journey of a thousand miles begins with just one step. The road to hope and healing begins the same way.

For those spiritually wounded from any circumstance in life, and for anyone who has ever wondered where God is in the sufferings and despair of human kind, please join me on my journey...

# Chapter One
## * * *

"Oh, little town of Bethlehem
How still we see thee lie
Above thy deep and dreamless sleep
The silent stars go by."
Voices of the carolers met the cold still air, enhancing the holiday spirit already prevalent in the city square. The scene never changed from year to year. The choir stood closely assembled in the bandstand area. The manger scene resided in its usual place on the west side of the park. A white star proudly topped the big fir tree, ablaze with bright multi-colored lights. Here and there a piece of wrapped candy could be found upon the ground, unsalvaged remnants from the parade of yesterday. Less than twenty-four hours ago, children and adults alike lined the streets of the north Georgia town of Marietta. Braving the cold, they had waited breathlessly for the final float bearing this year's first glimpse of Santa. Little children squealed with delight as he approached, while Santa waved with one hand and scattered candy into the crowd with the other as he rode by.

It was a tranquil time in 1952. Whole neighborhoods knew each other, and people felt a strong sense of community spirit. Most of Marietta's working population were employed by Lockheed Aircraft Corporation, the cornerstone on which the growing town was built.

"We hear the Christmas angels

1

The great, glad tidings tell.
O come to us, abide with us,
Our Lord Immanuel!"

The reverent hush that befell the listening crowd ended as the choir wrapped up their performance for that night. Families broke away and continued their holiday stroll. Most families made it an annual tradition to go downtown and see the Christmas decorations. Invariably, everyone would recognize someone and exchange greetings, maybe pausing for a brief conversation.

I was three years old in 1952, and I loved this magical time of year. It ranked right up there next to Easter and the family reunion. During these times my mother smiled a lot and seemed genuinely proud of us kids. If she chanced to meet someone she had not seen in quite some time, she would summon her children around her to show us off. I was a very insecure child who always stayed no more than an arm's length away from my mother in a crowd such as this, but my older brother wandered as far away as he could.

My father hated crowds and chose not to accompany us on these annual excursions. Mamma said he preferred to "stay home and drink himself into oblivion." My mother dressed us warmly, made a last effort to persuade Daddy to go, then regretfully left him alone as she loaded her three children into the car. Once out of his presence, however, her mood always brightened, and anticipation replaced the despair that had engulfed her only moments before.

She appeared to know everyone in town, and she seemed anxious to see just how many faces she could recognize. Carol from Pat-A-Cake bakery, Joe from the graveyard shift at the toy company where she worked. (She would never have spoken to any man if Daddy had been with us, but I never could understand why.) We saw the nurse from Dr. Alden's office, but Mama carefully avoided speaking to her. Dr. Alden had delivered my little brother almost a year before and Mama still had not paid him any money for his services. She guided us in another direction before any eye contact could be made. This move brought us face to face with a sweet looking couple who seemed at once happy to see us.

"Oh, kids, you remember Mattie and Larry Brach who used to go to our church, don't you?" On and on she would go, briefly introducing us before dismissing us from the conversation with her "children should be seen and not heard" attitude. I loved being included in the introductions even though, moments later, I wouldn't remember either names or from where we knew them.

My family, our neighbors, and people from church comprised my world. My family consisted of my mother, my father, an older brother, Micah, and Randy, the baby. Micah was only two and a half years older than me, but he was so much wiser. At least, that's what he said.

I was almost grown before I realized his mouth was much bigger than his brain. I considered Randy *my* baby and cared for him with tender devotion. Daddy's daily bouts with drunkenness gave rise to episodes of violence which made life miserable for all of us. He ignored everyone unless he wanted someone to torment. My mother's intense religious fervor and perverse sense of loyalty kept her bound to my father, which in turn, kept us exposed to continual abuse from both of them.

We were one of the poorest families in the neighborhood, more from mismanagement than lack of income. Too young to fully understand Mamma's accusation that Daddy "drank up all the money", I still somehow knew we were different. I felt the sting of inferiority.

When I played, I played alone, quietly entertaining myself as unobtrusively as possible in an effort to avoid being the object of my parents' rage. They rarely allowed me to go outside the house, and I was very lonely.

Most of the time I lived in an entirely different world, my world of imagination. Karen did not exist there, at least not the Karen crippled by shyness. In my private little world of fantasy I changed my name to Angela. I imagined myself to be a chatterbox, constantly surrounded by lots of friends my age. They always invited me to stay overnight, so I was rarely home. My friends enjoyed playing dress-up with my wardrobe because I had so many beautiful clothes with coordinating shoes and accessories. Since I so generously shared everything I owned, no one was envious but simply content to play with me. Oh, I was something in my imaginary world! I did know it was imaginary, though. I was painfully aware of my inadequacies in the real world, but I planned to be everything Angela represented when I grew up.

In reality I did have two friends. Teresa lived in the white house next door, and Janet lived in the red house on the other side of me. Teresa and I were the same age, and she had two sisters who often joined us in our play. I envied everything about those girls except they had to take a nap every afternoon. My mother dismissed that ritual by saying she could never get any of her children to go to sleep at night, much less in the daytime.

Truth is, we were afraid to sleep. Who knew what terrors the night would bring? If we were vigilant, if we sat in the dark with our eyes wide open, we could be forewarned of the dangers that were sure to come.

Janet was two years older than I and an only child. Her home represented my idea of heaven. Her mother stayed home and took good care of her. They had a new car and a boat. Supper was served at the same time every evening, and at times I was privileged to be invited to eat some of the best food I ever tasted. At their table, I was introduced to fried shrimp. If ambrosia was the food of the gods, it is only because the gods never tasted Mrs. Jones' fried shrimp. My mother said buying shrimp was a waste of money. She said if Mrs. Jones had three kids to feed instead of one she would learn real quick how to shop more economically for groceries. I was careful from then on to eat only two or three shrimp, even though I could easily have eaten the entire platter.

Personally, I thought it very smart of Mr. and Mrs. Jones to have only one child since, like us, they had only two bedrooms in their house. Some of our neighbors were fortunate enough to have three bedrooms, but the biggest difference in the tract houses on our street was the color of the slate siding. I thought it a very pretty neighborhood, each house distinguished by its pastel signature. Soft shades of yellow, green, blue, and gray, interspersed with white and tan, made it a pleasant street. Janet's house was the only dark one and it was my favorite. I'm sure the occupants and not solely the muted red color made it my choice. Nonetheless, I always thought it the prettiest, with the big shade tree in their front yard and the two-foot-high white, wooden fence separating their property from ours.

Our adjoining properties formed a gentle slope divided by the short white fence. Janet and I loved to get a running start at her driveway and run across her front yard, climb over the fence, and circle around my yard to repeat the process. She had always been a great playmate. Lately, though, she often felt too tired to run, so we had to play quietly.

Everyone said she might have more energy after the doctor fixed her heart. Grownups talked in hushed tones about the seriousness of the operation Janet would soon have. I was still too young to understand that she was "never going to be normal" and that she "wasn't quite right". I did not know, as her parents did, that she had a rare, progressively debilitating disease that they expected would claim her life before the age of ten, or that if she lived she would be severely retarded and physically handicapped. And so we played together contentedly, neither of us realizing she was living on borrowed time.

Her house offered me a happy reprieve, and I loved Janet and her mother. I spent every possible stolen moment there. Mrs. Jones spoke to me and Janet as though she really cared about us. My mother seemed to be extremely jealous of Mrs. Jones and forbade me to go there unless it was for her own convenience or perhaps when Mrs. Jones requested I come to play with Janet, and Mamma couldn't think of a reasonable way to refuse her.

In my daydreams, I was Janet's sister and her parents were mine. I was afraid of men, so I kept a wary eye on Mr. Jones. Unlike my father, he never touched me or gave me a reason to be afraid of him, but I watched him just in case. Like most people, the Joneses thought my father took better care of me than my mother did. That's because they couldn't see what really went on.

Lester Carter was so smooth, so charismatic with his dark, handsome looks and easy manner. He was tall and slender with dark, wavy hair - quite the ladies' man when my mother was not around. Drinking was his downfall. He kept his supply in the basement, because Mamma never allowed any liquor to be brought inside our house. She had her teetotaller image to protect. So well did she keep the secret that most of the neighbors did not find out until a few years later that Daddy had a drinking problem. He differed from my mother in that I could always coerce him into letting me go to Janet's house. Of course I had to do something for him in return, but I never saw it as a trade off, since I would have had to do what he wanted anyway.

Mama just said, "You have lots of things you could be doing here instead." I dreaded growing older. It seemed each new day she taught me how to do a new chore. Once I knew how to perform the task, she expected me to do it without being told, adding it to an already overwhelming list.

I wondered why she didn't let me rock the baby to sleep while she did the chores. She did the housework neater than I did, and I was better than her at rocking the baby to sleep. She said I was too little, but when we stuffed a pillow under my arm to support Randy's head and my arm, he would laugh and squeal in my lap as I rocked and held his bottle in his mouth. Finally, his eyes would flutter and his happy, gurgling sounds and waving arms would give way to yawns and little scratching noises as he softly flicked his fingernails back and forth across the raised ounce markings on the glass bottle.

When Mamma rocked him, he just seemed to scream and fight sleep forever, probably because she would periodically yell at me across the room to do whatever I was doing better or faster. Maybe the baby just didn't share her love of soap operas, which she watched religiously several hours a day. The house could have burned down around her during that time, and she would not have noticed. She seemed to be able to rock and ignore Randy crying by simply turning up the volume on the television set. Randy responded by turning up his own volume. It didn't make sense to me. I hated all the noise; the crying baby, the television, the dogs barking inside the house, my mother's raised voice. When I'm big, I'm going to play quiet music in my house all the time, I thought, and I won't let my babies cry.

I once questioned my mother as to why my older brother never had to help clean up. "Because he's not here," she replied.

"He's never here," I whined. "He always plays outside. Why does he get to play?"

"Because he's out of my hair, and anyway, housework is not for menfolks."

"Why not?" My inquisitive mind wanted to explore that idea.

"Because it just isn't. Now hush and get those clothes folded. You don't have all day." She closed the discussion with a look that said it would be in my best interest not to pursue the subject further.

I was already developing resentment toward my older brother, not directly with him, but with the preferential treatment he received from Mamma. She believed that women were on earth to serve men and beyond that had no purpose for existing. That is, until she had "served" more that she could stand. Then she would explode with all the vehemence of Old Faithful, spewing accusations and insults hotter than steam from that famous geyser.

Micah had equal reason to resent me. Jealous of the devotion Daddy seemingly lavished upon me, Micah had no way of knowing that I did not want Daddy's attention, or just how much that attention cost me. No matter how hard Micah tried, he could not get on Daddy's good side if, in fact, the man had a good side. When I did not hate Micah, I felt sorry for him. He worked so hard to receive a compliment or reward from our father. Instead, he received criticism and cruel treatment. Daddy beat Micah with a belt, his fist, a stick from the yard, or whatever was within his reach. Like a lonely puppy, Micah kept coming back for more. Each time he hoped for a pat on the back for picking up the trash in the yard, cutting the grass without mowing over something he shouldn't, or straightening up the basement clutter. Our parents' vocabulary did not include words of praise. Instead of the affirmation he sought, my brother was, at best, ignored. Most often he was beaten down with angry words and threats before he was physically beaten.

"Who told you to cut that grass?" my father would demand. "Git over here and let me see if I can knock some sense into you!" or "What were you doing in the basement? I thought I told you to stay out of places you don't belong.

You're in for a whippin' you won't soon forget." I don't know if Micah ever forgot or not, but I never did. The animal-like sounds Micah made each time he was struck repeated themselves in my head at night and awakened me to relive the beatings in my memory.

Beatings were a way of life in our house. Soon after my third birthday, I began weekly visits to a urologist, during which more pain and confusion were inflicted on my body and my psyche. Dr. Weaver was a kindly man who always called me "honey". His hands and voice were soft and gentle, but his instruments were as hard and cruel as the ones Daddy used when he played doctor.

Dr. Weaver tried to explain the necessity of stretching my urethra three times during each visit. I screamed "no" repeatedly, which was my way of explaining that the stinging pain coupled with the shame of having my most private parts exposed to two nurses, the doctor, and my mother was more than I could bear.

The horrible burning sensation repeated itself the first time I urinated after each visit to the doctor. I knew I must eventually give in to my biological demands, but I couldn't force myself into the pain. I fought the urge to urinate until I could fight no longer. I would sit forever on the toilet seat, clutching the towel bar on my right side. I was far too small for my feet to reach the floor, and so my legs dangled precariously, clutching the slippery peach colored porcelain as best they could. I fought for just the right balance to keep from leaning too far forward and falling off the toilet or leaning too far backward and slipping into the cold, germ ridden water.

On one such occasion, I received the worst beating I ever had from my mother. "Have you finished peeing yet?" she demanded after she entered the bathroom and closed the door behind her. I knew I was in trouble again because she gripped Daddy's leather belt in her hand.

"No," I answered.

"I'll give you five more minutes and you be better be done!"

I knew I could not deal with her and the pain already present in my body. I tried not to scream as the hot liquid finally broke free and cascaded down my legs and onto the floor while I stiffened and arched my back against the pain.

On her return, she found me frantically trying to clean the floor before she could discover what I had done.

"Forget about the floor," she said, jerking me up by the arm. "You've got some explaining to do. The doctor said you've been sticking things up yourself and causing damage to your insides. Now I want to know what you've been sticking up yourself and why in God's name you would do something like that!"

My eyes fell to the floor and I could feel my face contorting in spastic muscle twitches.

"Answer me, before I beat you 'til you can't see straight! What have you been sticking up yourself?"

"Nothing."

"Then who has?"

"Nobody."

I felt the first blows of the belt connect on my shoulder and then my head and face.

"Do you mean to tell me the doctor is lying!" she screeched as she landed more blows across my back and buttocks. I began to beg her to stop and promised to be good.

"So you admit you did it," she yelled in between blows.

"No, but I'll be good," I pleaded.

"You lying sack of shit! I'll teach you to tell the truth if it's the last thing I ever do." The full force of her anger, and her inability to hear the truth if I had chosen to tell, landed on my body as I lay face down on the cold bathroom tile with its foul odors penetrating my nostrils.

In the blind trust of childhood, I took my mother's words at face value. So the doctor was not my friend after all! Why would he betray me like that? Why would he think any child would hurt herself? It did not occur to me that my mother could or would twist the doctor's words to suit herself. It was easier for her to blame the victim, however young and innocent, than investigate the problem and accept the truth of her findings.

It is true that my father never bruised the outside of my body. My mother did that. On the other hand, Daddy greeted me with far different words. His favorite, uttered in that sickening, crooning voice he used only with me was, "Ride to the store with me, Kayron, and I'll buy you a candy bar." This always infuriated my older brother. He felt cheated by his father and jealous of me. Of course, that line from Daddy was a command rather than an invitation to me. If I really whined and protested, he promised me a Coke. Outwardly, he sounded like an indulgent father soothing a petulant child. Only I understood it was a sickening promise of sexual assault.

The doctor said I should be allowed to have Coke only on very special occasions. I soon learned that to my father "very special occasions" meant when someone was around to see. It seemed he liked getting credit for spoiling his only daughter. Daddy loved hearing someone say that he just couldn't bear to deprive his little girl of anything she wanted. In private, he used those exact words to try to tease and taunt me into sexual episodes. Offering me a Coca-Cola now served as a private threat after the episode in the woods the summer before.

Standing in the hallway of our house, he had rubbed his private parts then and said, "Daddy wasn't able to give you what you wanted yesterday since someone hung around here all day and all night. Now. Tell Daddy what you want."

"I want to go play with Janet," I said, knowing all the time my feeble attempts to avoid him were useless.

"You can play with her after you get finished here. You have to play with me first." He had wrapped my hair around his fist until it pulled. "Now what do you want Daddy to do?"

"I want you to go away!" I thought. I wished I could say what I was thinking. How could I answer him? It was a hard decision for a three-year-old. He tightened his grip on my hair.

"I want you to leave me alone!" I spat the words at him.

"Well, since you're so spunky this afternoon, we'll just do everything." I knew that meant it would really hurt, and I would be locked in his room afterward so I couldn't run away. No one was home now except the baby crying in the next room.

"I'll be right back," he said. He didn't bother to zip his pants as he walked to the kitchen to gather his supplies he used when he played doctor with me. I knew Daddy would get angry, but I had to try to quiet the baby. Standing on tiptoes, I reached into Randy's crib and patted him. Seeing me, he wailed even louder, wanting to be picked up.

"Shhh!" I said softly. I turned and saw my father standing naked in the doorway. I felt panic rising, choking the air from my chest.

"He wants his bottle." My voice was barely audible.

"Then fix him one, and get in your mamma's bed!" he roared.

I watched him disappear to his room, and I could hear the clink of glass and metal as he set up various household objects he used on me when he played doctor. I could smell rubbing alcohol, and I could feel without feeling it the stinging pain between my legs.

The warm May breezes seemed to caress my face as I ran. I did not remember leaving the house, but I found myself already two blocks away. I did not remember falling either, but blood trickled down my legs, seeping around the gravel embedded in my knees. I had no way of knowing if Daddy followed me, but I could not run any farther. My chest hurt and I could not take a deep breath.

I'll feel better when I get to my water, I thought. My brother had taken me with him once when he ran away. Not far into the woods, we had crossed a small stream where water tumbled over rocks, and I was intrigued by the sound and the soft moss covering the ground beneath the trees. It became my special place. My father had never found me there. Just thinking about it made me feel better. I leaned my back against a tree and closed my eyes for a moment to catch my breath. Soon my racing heart slowed to a more normal pace, and I lingered there with my eyes shut tight against the world.

A searing pain told me I was caught. Daddy's crushing grip encased my hand, and I did not attempt to pull it free. Instead, I concentrated on suppressing the scream that wanted to escape. Daddy could not tolerate crying.

"Where are you going?" he asked with mock concern. "I was worried about you." He held my hand loosely and continued speaking as we walked toward two ladies gossiping at the edge of the street. "Daddy will take you anywhere you want to go, Sweetheart, but you must never leave our yard by yourself." He raised my hand slightly and bent down to plant a gentle kiss on my fingertips in an effort to impress the ladies.

One of the ladies smiled and said, "You found her! She's all right, I trust?"

"Yep! She said she just wanted to go for a walk. She can't seem to understand that something bad could happen to her when she wanders off. I said I was going to spank her when I found her, but I'm so relieved she's okay I just can't bring myself to punish her." Everyone laughed. Everyone except me. I knew I would get far worse than a spanking.

"Good day ladies." With a pleasant smile on his face, Daddy walked toward home, still holding my hand and whistling an upbeat tune. I walked silently beside him, staring straight ahead, my mouth clenched into a stoic line.

"Poor man. He must have been worried sick," I heard one of the women sympathize. When we reached home, Daddy instructed me to get into the car.

"Can I just go in the house and see if Randy is still crying?" I begged. He ignored my childish plea, and one look into his demonic eyes silenced any further attempt to check on the baby. We rode two blocks to the little neighborhood grocery store where he purchased one small bottle of Coke.

In total silence, he drove about two miles to a narrow graveled road. I felt my stomach giving birth to feelings of dread. They would crawl up my chest and snatch away my breath until they reached my brain and I wouldn't be able to think anymore. I hated this road. There were never any other cars there. Besides, I always scratched my legs on the briars when he dragged me through the blackberry bushes and on past the undergrowth of weeds to get deeper into the woods. He parked the car as far to the right side of the road as he could. Then he took a bottle opener from the glove compartment and the Coke. "Come on!" he demanded, motioning me to follow out the driver side.

When Daddy was satisfied that we were far enough from the road, he sat down on the ground. I remained standing. "You're awfully quiet," he remarked cheerfully. "Are you thirsty?" I didn't answer. It was a trick. Did he think I was stupid? I wasn't a dumb little kid anymore! I was three and a half and I had learned not to anticipate anything good from him because he always disappointed me. Of course I was thirsty! The sun beamed down hot as blue blazes, and running had left my throat dry and parched. He made a ceremony of taking the cap off the bottle, talking about the heat of the day and the coldness of the drink as he relaxed in the cool of the trees.

"Daddy gets the first drink." He took a long swig, leaving about three fourths for me. Then he unzipped his pants. He

14

urinated just a little into the coke bottle, then aimed into the bushes to finish relieving himself. "The rest is for you," he said, handing me the bottle. When I refused to drink, he grabbed my head and pushed the entire top of the bottle into my mouth. He poured it down my throat, forcing me to swallow or strangle. I managed to do a little of both and hoped this would be all he would require of me. I burped and wanted to throw up, but I saw the stormy darkness in his eyes and brought my stomach muscles under control.

His pants were still unzipped. He sailed the nearly empty bottle backwards over his head and reached his other hand under my chin at the same time. I tried to avoid his eyes. They frightened me. "Look at me," he crooned. My eyes met his because they had no choice. "You know what daddy likes," he continued. He stood facing me, his erect penis at my face level. I thought he smelled like the elephant at the zoo, and I turned my head away. I hated the smell almost as much as I hated the way he tasted. Suddenly, I remembered the baby and wondered if he could really starve to death before I got home. Mamma often said I was going to let him starve to death, and he had not been fed since this morning. My immense concern for Randy forced me to finish the oral sex without any more hesitation.

I could see Micah playing in the front yard as we pulled into the driveway. My mother should be home from work. It was late evening. Before I could even climb out of the car, I heard my mother screaming at my father from the porch. "Where have you been? You've been out drinking again, haven't you?"

"Now, Rose. Calm down. She run away again," he explained, jabbing a thumb in my direction. "I think she's ruined another dress, too. You better get this kid of yours under control!" The last time I had come home with Daddy with snags in my dress, he told Mamma he had found me picking blackberries. She assumed I had been there again. She did not see a defenseless little girl with bleeding legs and a devastated spirit.

"What do you mean going off and leaving the baby all alone? You want him to starve to death?" Her anger was directed at me, not the one I thought responsible for Randy's negligent condition. "I come in from working all day and you haven't set the table or fed the baby or nothin'," she continued. "You been out feedin' your own face. You think God put those blackberries there just for you? Get in this house! After supper I'm going to beat you 'til your nose bleeds!" She always said that, and sometimes she did. I didn't worry about it that night though. Daddy had settled into a happy mood, and the baby played peacefully on a pallet on the living room floor. I thought Daddy would probably talk Mamma into going to bed early with him, and he would play games with her.

But that was last summer. A lot had happened since then. No longer a tiny baby, Randy could now crawl and hold his own bottle. He loved to stand in his crib and hold onto the bars for balance while he bounced up and down. He was a sweet baby, and he laughed a lot. I wished I could be little like him, because Daddy ignored him and Mama played with him a lot. I envied Micah most of all, because he started school this year, and he stayed there almost all day long. I didn't know what school was, but whatever it was, I liked it better than being home with Daddy.

Micah complained about first grade. He told me it was real hard work. "You're lucky you don't have to go," he assured me. "You're probably going to fail first grade when you do, 'cause it's really hard for me, and I'm a lot smarter than you are," he said.

"I'm never going to fail anything," I told him. "I'm going to make better grades than you do. You'll see!" I didn't worry about school. I was convinced anything Micah could do, I could do better.

# Chapter Two
## * * *

Mamma woke us early the morning after we went downtown to see the holiday decorations. Granny was coming to spend Christmas with us. She would be arriving on the Trailways bus at noon, and lots of cleaning had to be done before then. Even Micah had chores to do this morning. Mamma may not have believed the male gender should have to do housework, but when she had too much to do and too little time in which to do it, the rules changed. Much to Micah's dismay, Mamma made him help also.

My first unspoken order of business was to strip the bed I slept in so it could dry out. Without fail, I discovered my mattress soaked each morning from several bedwetting episodes during the night. I awoke shivering, and I knew that meant the pilot had blown out on the floor furnace while we slept. The one in the living room rarely gave us any trouble. The furnace in the hall, which was supposed to provide heat for the bedrooms, was another story. It seemed programmed to break on a regular basis and leave us defenseless against the bitter winter chill.

Mamma fussed and swore as she went out the back door and down the steps, making her way to the basement to relight the uncooperative furnace. I stood in the bathroom half dressed and held my hands over my ears to drown out my mother's angry noises. She was almost directly below me yelling at the furnace as if she expected it to understand and obey her. For good measure, she struck it several times with something that made a terrible clanging sound.

By that time, I had managed to pull my dress over my head and put on clean panties and socks. Rubbing the sleep from my eyes, I made my way to the warmer part of the house, pausing in the dining room to yawn and lean my head against the telephone table. I really did not mind this particular mishap too much because Mamma usually took pity on me and held me in her lap near the working source of heat until we both warmed up. A pan of water already sat on the edge of the grate with a washcloth and bar of soap nearby. Mamma would bathe me from the waist down to help dissipate the smell of dried urine that followed me everywhere I went. She was not a particularly clean person by most folks' standards, and she considered a morning bath a real waste of water. We took baths every other night in the winter time. She bathed the baby first. Since I was the next cleanest, she allowed me to have my bath after Randy. Micah bathed after me in the same water.

This was not to be one of those mornings of waking up slowly in Mamma's lap. I was still dozing against the telephone table when I heard her saying, "Git that rag and wash yourself off." Mamma always referred to washcloths as rags, which in our household was probably a more accurate description. At the sound of her voice, I yawned again and rallied to consciousness. I wanted to enjoy this special day.

"How long before Granny gets here?" I asked as Mamma buttoned my dress.

"She'll be here at lunch time," she said. "Right now it's time for breakfast."

Mamma was in a pleasant mood, now that the gas was flowing properly again. A pan of grits sat uncovered on the stove. A dry film began forming atop the cooked cereal while the eggs waited on a nearby counter to be fried or scrambled.

The pile of dough in an adjacent bowl waited its turn to be hand rolled into individual biscuits. The oven's magic heat had not yet transformed it into something edible. Mamma cooked the eggs as soon as the biscuits were in the oven. By the time our bread was cooked, though, the grits were stone cold and so firm you could have sliced through them with a knife. She tried to make them edible again by stirring cold water into the mixture and reheating it. Lukewarm, lumpy grits, greasy eggs, and biscuits. Every morning, same menu. I tried to avoid breathing the eggs' aroma. They turned my stomach. I covered the ones on my plate with grits. Probably it was not so much the eggs as it was the grease in which they were cooked. Mamma saved the grease drippings from bacon to fry with so she wouldn't have to buy shortening or oil at the grocery store. I couldn't tolerate the grits' texture.

"If you're not going to eat your food, give it to the dogs," Mamma was saying. Good. She was not going to force the issue of eating everything on my plate today. "But don't let me hear you saying you're hungry before lunch is ready," she hollered after me as I slid away from the table.

The floors still had to be swept and mopped and all the bed linens changed. We did only the most cursory housecleaning on a regular basis in our home. Even a thorough mopping of the floors occurred only when we expected company. I liked cleaning the bathroom best. Of all the rooms, that one produced the most noticeable improvement in the shortest length of time. I had learned to sprinkle just the right amount of powdered cleanser to remove the brown scum that covered the bottom half of the tub. Mamma still had to measure for me the amount of liquid cleanser I needed to scrub the floor and toilet. Dirty clothes and towels lay strewn all over the small area and had to be carried to the clothes basket in the hall closet before any cleaning could be done. That was easy and already the bathroom looked better.

It took a lot longer to straighten all the things on the tray on the back of the commode and the three shelves above it. Mamma never threw anything away. She just relocated it to another spot in the house. Bottles of all sizes, mostly empty, fought for shelf space with Daddy's shaving equipment, shampoo, twisted toothpaste tubes, and other personal care items. There lay an occasional first aid item; an unwrapped spool of gauze, some antibacterial solution with its lid missing, and an Ace bandage, unrolled and tangled with everything else.

Mamma kept a close eye on the clock as the time drew near for Granny's arrival. She called a halt to the housecleaning in plenty of time to meet her bus. It stopped at a little grocery store on Highway 41 just a mile from our house on its way to the bus station downtown. Mamma liked to be there when the bus pulled in, so Granny would not have to wait. She didn't get any argument from us kids. My mother's mother was the greatest joy in our lives. She lived outside Eufaula, Alabama, a good seven hour journey in our old station wagon, over mostly two-lane, narrow roads with enough pot holes to keep the driver from falling asleep during the trip. Sometimes Granny's other daughter, my Aunt Helen, would bring Granny to our house. At other times, Granny rode up on the train from Columbus to Atlanta and we would pick her up there.

She rarely brought treats or presents for us when she came to visit. She didn't need to. Her presence was enough excitement for both Micah and me. We stood on a two-foot-high retainer wall at the edge of the parking lot, craning our necks for the first glimpse of her arrival. Because Micah was taller he could see the bus coming a block away, a fact that irritated me highly. It wasn't fair that I should get the knowledge second hand, especially when it came from my biggest rival. I recovered quickly, though. Sometime between my first glimpse and the time it pulled into its assigned stopping place, we both started hopping up and down with excitement.

Exhaust fumes from the huge vehicle formed gray vapors that whorled into the cold December air, a visual backdrop to the engine's loud roar. We waited impatiently for the door to swing open. Soon we were rewarded with Granny's five-foot-two skeletal frame slowly emerging onto the top step. The driver in his crisp uniform and official looking cap stepped out first and offered her his hand as she dismounted. Granny lived simply and traveled light. She brought only herself and a few changes of clothes in an old suitcase with a broken clasp. A man's discarded belt buckled around the suitcase held it together. The driver wished her a happy visit with her grandchildren and a Merry Christmas. "Don't you spoil them younguns too much now. Remember their Mamma's got to live with them after you go home!" he admonished. Granny had obviously told him probably more that he cared to hear on the long ride.

Micah carried her suitcase to our car for her, showing her how much stronger he was now that he had turned six in September. We didn't make it to the car before Granny deluged us with hugs and kisses. "Come here and let me hug yore neck!" she said to each of us in turn. "I couldn't wait for that old bus to get here so I could see my babies!" Granny knew nothing about the study of psychology. She just loved us in her natural, easy-going way. We were important to her and we knew it.

"How's Granny's little man?" she asked as she lifted Randy from Mamma's arms and encased him in a warm embrace.

I wanted to hear stories about Granny's trip. She always told us interesting things that happened during the journey. She would be able to tell anything one might want to know about the person in the seat next to her, for sure, and probably she could tell you quite a bit about several others in the same bus. She got to know all the children on board and gave pieces of

21

candy or sticks of gum to them if there were only a few. Fussy ones who were cranky from the confining ride were offered a place in Granny's lap, much to the relief of weary mothers. Granny knew a different face and change of scenery was sometimes all it took to calm a fretful baby.

I had to know what the children were wearing, and Granny would delight in describing every little detail to me. Equally important to me were their names. I could tell a lot about a person by their name. Or so I thought. I liked sweet sounding names, so all the Amys and Cindys and Melanies were likable children. Marthas and Diannes and Carolyns must be hard to get to know because their names sounded formidable to me. I was sure I would not like them very much. Jennifer sounded elegant, as did Melissa. Therefore, they were interesting. Debbies, Peggies, and Patties couldn't be much fun. There were simply too many of them. The one thing I liked about myself was my name. Karen. Simple. Not overly common in my neck of the woods, yet not unusual enough to evoke much comment. It could have been worse. The only thing I would have changed it to would have been Angela or Amy or maybe Alison. I liked "A" names. They sounded friendly.

I liked my name, I should say, when it was pronounced correctly. My father never pronounced it right. He even spelled it "Kayron" just the way he said it. My mother at times had trouble saying it so that it sounded right to her. I never knew if it would come out "Kayrin", or more like one syllable. Granny almost always called me Katie, and that was fine, too. It was hard to mispronounce Katie.

So Granny gave us the facts about her trip and my imagination spun wonderful webs of fantasy to make it more interesting. We talked as Granny peeled potatoes to boil for supper. Mamma always cut up the chicken. We children weren't allowed to handle knives. Mamma was very emphatic about that. As a toddler, I had nearly severed my finger with a butcher knife when Mamma went to the next apartment to use their phone. As a result of the experience and Mamma's subsequent reminders that knives can kill you, I had developed a deep fear of the shiny, pointed objects. I kept my fear to myself, though. I knew that if Daddy knew I was scared he would threaten me with them, and Mamma would just call me a baby. So I pretended I wasn't afraid of knives by always asking if I could cut up the chicken, knowing the answer would be, "No. Don't touch that knife!"

So Mamma cut the chicken and Granny did whatever needed to be done that I couldn't do. A lot of preparation went into the evening meal. Granny's visit and Christmas being just a few days away made it a special time. Mamma believed in baking holiday goodies, and we believed in eating anything with sugar in it. Granny's presence seemed to give Mamma an automatic dose of patience. She allowed us to help her make the cakes and pies to be enjoyed later on.

The two of them caught up on the news from both sides of the river, as they liked to say, referring to the Chattahoochee River that divides Georgia from Alabama. Mostly that day they talked about my stay in the hospital a few months back. Granny wasn't clear on some things, and she wanted more explanation. I tried not to listen. Tried not to let their words bring back to life the terror of being alone in the hospital. Most of it went over my head anyway. I only understood that Dr. Weaver wanted to "take a look and see what's going on up there" so he could fix my bladder. I knew they had discovered I had one kidney instead of two, and that it was in the wrong place.

"Well, if the doctor did everything he could that needed to be done, why does she still hurt when she goes to the bathroom?" Granny wanted to know. Mamma didn't know either. My mother had a strange reverence about doctors. She figured if he wanted her to know something, he would tell her.

She asked no questions of them. She repeated to Granny what she already knew about how many times a week, and for how long I would have to continue to see him in his office. Mamma did not tell her she left me clinging to her skirts as the nurse pulled me away to put me in a ward with seven other children. She didn't tell her I felt so scared at being left alone in that pristine world of antiseptic smells and hard cement block walls with its thick shiny coats of pale green paint that I screamed hysterically until a nurse slapped me to keep me from upsetting the other patients.

Maybe Mamma didn't even know I was embarrassed when some other children asked, "Why are you here?" when she first brought me to the room and she told them the doctor was going to operate on the parts inside that help me go pee-pee. The children looked immediately to my midsection, grateful, I'm sure, that they were just having their tonsils out.

Going to the hospital had not helped anyway. I still wet my pants day and night. By the time I realized I had to go, I had already gone. Most of the time Mamma was very patient with me, but sometimes she said I just wasn't trying hard enough.

Granny said, "I just don't understand why Karen is still going to him if he has done everything he knows to do and she still ain't no better off." She added, "I think yore puttin' her through a lot of unnecessary stuff." Granny presented her closing argument on that subject, and I felt relieved. It was beginning to get heated in the kitchen and not just from the stove's heat.

It seemed Micah could run on raw energy forever, but my body became tired and ready for bed several hours before bedtime. So it was a great comfort when Granny told me to come get in her lap for a while. "Somebody's got a birthday comin' up soon," she said. "Granny's little angel is purty near four years old. Sometimes I could near 'bout swear I see a halo above yore little blond curls."

I gave her a sleepy smile and a yawn. I didn't want to go to sleep. For I knew when sleep overtook me, she would put me to bed, and a whole day of her visit would be gone.

"Quit squirmin' around, Katie. Lie back and let me hold you a little bit." Granny's gentle encouragement stilled my restlessness. I could not fight against Granny. Never could. And so we rocked as she and Mamma talked. All too soon I drifted away into another land, safe in Granny's arms.

# Chapter Three
## * * *

My mother had very strict, albeit very confused, religious convictions. I never knew from whence came her unlimited store of sidetracked ideas. My grandmother did not share her views, although Granny did have a few old superstitions of her own she chose to cling to. Mamma lived and breathed by the belief that the poorer and more unhappy a person was, the closer he was to God. Nothing could have been further from the teachings of Jesus, but somehow she had adopted that creed. She taught us, therefore, to eke out a living, but not to have any excess, so that we would not be tempted to be satisfied with ourselves. If we had anything more than the bare necessities of life, we should give it to someone less fortunate than us. More damaging than that, Mamma taught us that if we had one moment of feeling good about ourselves we needed to confess that sin before God so that pride would not bring about our downfall.

Daddy forced us to eat everything on our plates, but whatever Daddy or Mamma did not eat was given to the dogs or saved for some other useful purpose. A half-eaten biscuit would be wrapped up until Saturday night. Then it would be used to shine my patent leather shoes before being thrown into the yard for some bird or our free-roaming chickens to eat. My mother recycled long before it became an environmental issue. There were starving children in China she said, so I had to eat all my food. Somehow the fate of a dying child halfway around the world rested on us eating all our food. I couldn't see the correlation, but I offered to send my food to China. Mamma rewarded me with a spanking. If I said I was not hungry, she said I was ungrateful. If we left a bite of food on our plate, Daddy would pile it high again and demand we eat all of it. I tried to not eat anything all day, hoping my stomach would hold whatever he required me to eat that evening.

I wondered why God didn't equal it out a little better. Mamma said overseas they would be grateful for anything and we certainly had more than we wanted, especially squash and butterbeans. I did not ask because people did not question God, and children did not question anything!

There was not much reason for living aside from going to church. We could not do anything that might be interpreted as fun, unless it was "family time". Now there was an exercise in futility. Time for the kids to fight with each other. Time for Mamma and Daddy to fight with each other. The only difference from our regular routine was the location, the most common being a nearby lake for a picnic. We always went away one week a year to do something together. Usually we visited Mama's relatives in Florida or Daddy's relatives in Louisiana.

A deck of cards was strictly forbidden in our house. That was too closely related to gambling. We could not go to the movies because that was sinful. Teresa and her sisters went sometimes. So did Janet. They would tell me all about wonderful works of art by a man named Walt Disney. I was invited to go with them by their mothers who explained to my mother that they were "clean" children's movies. My mother said the same theater also showed dirty movies and her children would not be seen there. So I heard secondhand about "Song of the South" and Uncle Remus, Haley Mills and "Polyanna".

They sounded a lot better than those stupid cartoons

Mamma did allow us to watch on TV. Popeye always fought with Brutus, and who would want that idiot Olive Oyl anyway? Proof positive that men will fight over anything. I became cynical at a very early age, but the cartoons backed up what I had already witnessed in life. In another popular cartoon, the bad guy tied the beautiful lady to the railroad track, making her dependent on another man to come along and rescue her from certain destruction. Then she gave her undying gratitude to her rescuer as he carried her away into the sunset.

I could not sit still for those kinds of shows. They were almost as dumb as my mother's soap operas, and they upset me in a way I did not understand. I was not old enough to analyze them for the sexist attitude they promoted, but it was precisely that message that sent me from the television set in search of something better to do.

Micah watched violent cartoons with feverish intensity. Then he incorporated ideas he got from them into his play, tying up his playmates and acting out his will to dominate, especially with girls or smaller or weaker children. On the other hand, he was very protective of me, playing the big brother role to the hilt. At times he would take the blame and punishment when my mother was bent on spanking me. Most of the time, I was so confused I did not understand why she wanted to spank me, or if Micah really was responsible for the incident. In any case, it took great courage for him to intercede on my behalf, and I was grateful. I viewed my big brother with mixed emotions. Mostly, I envied the fact that he had a life outside our house.

I waged an active campaign to go to school. It was the only feasible plan I could devise that would buy me time away from Daddy. I had heard other mothers talking about their children starting school early even though they weren't quite old enough yet. I didn't know the whys and wherefores of their particular situations. I just knew there had to be a way I could go too. I simply could not endure another year of waiting.

I made my mother the target of a heavy offensive battle that I refused to give up until she relented. I would turn six January 10th. The rule stated I had to be six years old by January 1st. She explained to me that since there were only nine days difference, I might be able to start this year instead of waiting another whole year. A short time later Mamma told me she had asked about me registering in the fall and the school said no.

"Well, when can I go?" I asked.

"Micah is going to be getting out of school for the summer soon. When he starts again this fall, you will have one more year to wait from that time." I couldn't grasp the concept of that much time, but it sounded like never to me.

Downhearted beyond description, I pleaded, "Could I just go with Micah every day and watch?" I cried with disappointment. My mother sympathized, puzzled that a child so shy and introverted would be so desperate to go to school.

I may as well have been drowning in the middle of the ocean, so deep was my despair. There had been a glimmer of hope in my bleak emotional state. Now, since all hope of going to school was gone, nothing remained to help me cope with Daddy.

Panic and a hot, sick feeling lived in my body making me slow and ill and quiet. My father's voice directed at me would sometimes either immobilize me or cause a sudden outburst of tears which I was powerless to control. I could no longer pretend the attacks were happening to "the other me". I had to get completely away. The "other me" materialized into a real personality who forced me out and occupied my consciousness when I no longer could.

My only escape depended on my ability to concentrate hard enough on a focal point to fall asleep. When I awoke my headache would be gone, but so would my energy. Then I would be subdued, and my mother would usually be congratulating herself on having finally beat some sense into me. I nursed my cuts and bruises, knowing she had put them there, but unable to recall being hit. She chastised me for being insolent, spiteful, sarcastic, and screaming, "I hate you". I didn't remember doing any of those things. She must be lying. But Mamma never lied. She was very particular about making sure she told the truth. Unless the subject concerned Daddy. She always lied about him.

Maybe I am crazy, I thought. Micah said so, but once I heard someone say that if you think you're crazy, you're not. They said really crazy people never think they are. If I wasn't crazy, why would my mother hit me when I was asleep? Was she crazy perhaps?

More and more frequently, time lapses occurred when I could not recall how I changed from being in one place with my father to being in another room with my mother. It took a few minutes to reorient myself and catch up on the lost time. I had no awareness of the other personality, which added to my confusion. The early stages of Multiple Personality Disorder were already forming.

For some reason I did not understand, Daddy changed the way he played the game. No longer intent on inflicting pain as his primary aim, he now determined that I should enjoy it with him and that my body should "respond". He began to do strange things that frightened me even more than when he played doctor. It didn't hurt so much anymore, but it did not feel good as he insisted it did. "You like it. You know you do. Tell Daddy you like for me to touch you there."

"I don't like it! I want to get up. Leave me alone," I begged.

"Okay. You do it then," he said as he took my finger and tried to teach me the fine art of masturbation. I refused to cooperate. He tried for many months before giving up, proclaiming that his only daughter was too stupid to even be a whore. The summer heat limited his desire to satisfying only himself. The game was not as horrible as it had been. More like Chinese water torture, I found waiting for him to finish to be the hardest part.

When the sexual assaults were not terribly painful, I could detach myself and daydream about more pleasant things. My Bible contained beautiful pictures of the Garden of Eden, and other places and people of interest. I knew all the corresponding stories from Sunday School, but I rewrote them in my mind during those times. By the time I changed that snake into a thousand butterflies, and threw the man out of the garden, and turned some of the plain green trees into flowering ones in full bloom, Daddy would be finished and I would be lying there with slimy, sticky gunk on my stomach and between my legs, and he would be walking away to the bathroom.

* * * * *

Sometime during that summer I heard of a new thing. Something called kindergarten. My friend next door, Teresa, said, "I might go, but I don't know if I really want to. I might just stay home with my sister."

"What is kindergarten?" I asked.

"Well, it's something like school, only more fun. You don't *have* to go to kindergarten and you have to pay for it if you do because it isn't free like school."

The idea of kindergarten drew me like a magnet, but if it cost money, I knew I didn't stand a chance. Teresa said it wasn't at the school. You went to kindergarten at church, but it wasn't the same as Vacation Bible School. I didn't much care what it was like. I wanted to go. I had to go.

I hounded my mother to no end over this issue and put her through every emotion known to mothers. She wanted to ignore me, but I wouldn't go away. She knew, as I didn't, that it was not a simple matter of her working harder and longer to earn money for something I wanted. She would have willingly done that. The biggest problem for her was going against Daddy. He was a mountain she could not climb, but I was a need that had to be met. Caught between a rock and a hard place, she did not know where to turn.

Occasionally Mamma would comment to me in private that she had called someone to locate a place that offered kindergarten, or that she was trying to find me a ride, or we couldn't afford it, but she would see if she could make some arrangements. Knowing she was trying kept hope intact and carried me through the long, hot summer. At long last, I received an answer to my nightly prayer that I couldn't say out loud, but added silently in my heart after I had said "Amen." I was hanging clothes on the clothesline in the backyard one day when my mother joined me and pretended to show me how to do it "right".

"Okay honey, I have something to tell you but you can't get excited. Your daddy might be looking out the window. I made arrangements for you to start kindergarten in two weeks, but you cannot tell anyone. If your daddy finds out about it, he won't let you go. I'll tell him when the time comes, but don't you say a word to him about it." I could keep secrets real good. For the first time, one held benefits for me, also. It became my secret weapon, this private knowledge to which Daddy was not privileged.

A week later my teacher-to-be called. I was too shy to talk to her on the phone, but my mother gave me the message that the teacher was looking forward to having me in her class. It was really going to happen! I couldn't believe it. It was the best news ever!

Mamma and Daddy worked opposite hours throughout most of my childhood, so one of them could be home with the children. Mamma didn't want to leave us alone for that long at a time if she could avoid it, and Daddy wanted ample opportunity to practice his sexual abuse without interruption.

I fought him over lying down with him the morning after my teacher called. I was still euphoric over kindergarten, whatever that was. Daddy wheedled and coaxed me into bed, but I couldn't come down from my cloud to wallow in his pit. It was just too far to fall. He plied me with my obligation of being his little girl.

"Well, I don't care! Pretty soon I'm going to kindergarten and then I won't have to lay down with you anymore!" I screamed at him.

He rolled off me and sat on the edge of the bed staring down at me. My unexpected announcement stunned him into silence. I had gone too far. Probably I had just blown my chance to go after all! Mamma would beat me for sure. She had gone to a lot of trouble to get me enrolled and come up with the tuition. She had also worked hard at keeping it a secret and I had just blurted it out.

"What's this I hear about Kayron going to school?" he asked Mamma when she called from work later that morning. A short conversation followed and then, "Well, I don't want to hear anymore such talk!" as he slammed down the phone.

"You ain't going nowhere," he said to me when he hung up. "Don't be telling lies to me. You had me worried to death." What was he worried about?

Nevertheless, I did start with the class that year. My mother, brothers, and I paid for the privilege, however. Daddy became ill-tempered and took out his anger on my little brother who no longer had me there to defend him. When Micah came home from school, Daddy beat him just because he was there. My father constantly berated my mother and made life more difficult for her whenever he could. As for me, my times of going to bed with him were fewer but harsher when they occurred. He always finished by inflicting pain somehow "to teach you a lesson and you know why" he would say. I learned that all privileges are bought with a price. I felt guilty that my family should suffer because of me, but I was still young enough to claim what I needed for my emotional survival - a practice I was to give up completely later in life.

Halfway through the school year, Mamma said I had to drop out. She said we just could not afford it anymore, but I knew she couldn't resist Daddy's insistence anymore. The teacher discouraged Mamma from removing me from class, saying I needed it more than any child she had ever seen. Mamma maintained a firm position and told her I would be leaving. Then the director called, saying the church would pay for my tuition. When Mamma claimed she had no way of getting me back and forth, the mother of one of my classmates insisted on picking me up and bringing me home, since she drove right past my house taking her son to school. Removing me at that point would have aroused suspicion, and they could not afford that. So it was decided that I could finish the year, but once again Daddy's anger sharpened to a razor's edge.

Mamma and Daddy had violent arguments which erupted into physical attacks between them. My mother screamed at him, "You can't keep her locked up in this house the rest of her life, Lester! People will wonder what's going on. She was going to have to start school sooner or later anyway!"

Later she would say to me, "Can't you just once be nice to your Daddy? He thinks the sun rises and sets on you and what thanks does he get? Ever since you were a little bitty thing you've screamed and fussed every time he got near you. When you learned to crawl, you crawled under the table to get away from him. How do you think that makes him feel?" It wasn't enough to know I was a bad kid. Now she wanted me to feel guilty for being a bad baby a few years back.

Daddy became more sullen and drank more frequently - straight vodka in his private basement hideaway. He looked hurt and rejected when I went next door to play. Sometimes he allowed me to go places for a few hours with the Joneses. At Christmas time my parents let me ride with Janet to see the lights and decorations in Atlanta. We rode through the ritzy part of town, past the governor's mansion and all his rich neighbors' houses. With my face glued to the car window, I tried to take it all in: reindeer flying into the air ready to lift off Santa's sleigh from the rooftop, Mary and Joseph kneeling in the hay beside the baby Jesus, carollers with their mouths open in song. I didn't want to miss a single display. It was so different than doing the same thing with my own family. In our car, I was embarrassed to look out the window, for fear someone might be looking back at me and know my shame.

I had unexpected privileges at times, and I never knew just exactly what brought about the change. Once I went on a shopping trip with Janet and her mother for Janet's new orthopedic shoes she had to be fitted for periodically. We finished the outing by stopping at the local drug store for something to drink. I had always wanted to sit on those intriguing round stools that turned all the way around in either direction. Had often wondered how it would feel to order something at that counter and sip cold liquid through a straw. Janet and I sat next to each other, gently twisting our seats side to side as we held onto the counter's edge for support. Janet enjoyed the simple pleasures of life, and I was discovering this one with her. A smile found its way to my lips and lingered there. Even the smile felt strange and different and wonderful.

Now that I was five and a half, I had developed a fighting spirit that could not be satisfied with meekly accepting life as it was handed to me. I was piteously passive to any observer, yet a cauldron of rebellion raged behind my stoic face. Curiosity bubbled like poison in a witch's pot, churning my brain with questions I was forbidden to ask. There *was* another side of life. I had seen evidence of good things which made me question the bad things. Not all parents acted like mine, and not all people thought it was wrong for children to wiggle and laugh. My mother would have slapped me for twisting on the drugstore stool. Mrs. Jones laughed and said it didn't take much to make us two happy. Why the difference? I became an ardent observer of people, and inadvertently, a people pleaser, changing my behavior, thoughts and wishes to suit whomever I was with.

I made more and more demands on my parents. Other children were allowed to go visit with their grandparents during the summer. Even Micah. Why couldn't I? That was out of the question, they said, but after many declined invitations, they did finally relent and allow me to go to the lake one Saturday with Janet.

"Remember to bring your bathing suit tomorrow," Mrs. Jones said.

"I don't have one," I answered.

"Well, that's all right. Just bring yourself then." I didn't tell her I was terrified of the water and I wouldn't get in it even if I did have a bathing suit.

On the way to the lake the next day, Janet handed me a sack. "We bought you something," she said, smiling. There was excitement in her voice.

"Pull it out of the sack and see if you like it," her mother said. I was dumbfounded to find they had bought me and Janet matching suits the night before. I must be dreaming. It was yellow, Janet's favorite color. I loved it. Like a spring garden bathed in sunlight, dainty printed flowers danced on the yellow material. It was a one-piece cotton outfit with a ruffle of tiny crimped pleats that would stand straight out when I spun around on one foot.

After a boat ride on the lake, we feasted on grilled hamburgers, potato salad, cantaloupe, and chocolate cake. Food had never tasted so good, each bite better than the one before. Perfect weather, delicious food, favorite friends, good fun, and peace of mind. I longed to close my eyes and lift my face to the gentle wind and the sun's warmth, to seal myself in a bubble of isolation in order to hold on to this wonderful day.

Sadly, my fears and insecurities made me too conscious of people being nearby. They might see me. They might laugh at me. Even worse I would not be able to see them. Someone might play a trick on me. Yet, so great was my desire to experience a moment of this day with my eyes closed that I concocted a plan to be able to do so without drawing attention to myself. Janet splashed in the water's edge with her father. Mrs. Jones was clearing the picnic table, sealing the unused food in plastic containers. I ran to her.

"Do you want me to throw the trash away for you?" I offered.

"Well, thank you!" she said. "That's very nice of you."

The trash container sat several yards away at the edge of the woods. With my back to everyone, I paused with my arms full of trash just above the garbage can. Seizing the moment, I closed my eyes and breathed deeply in an effort to fill my senses with the treasures of nature. I was disappointed to smell only old garbage and hear the threatening buzz of a bumblebee.

Oh, well. It doesn't really matter, I thought.

How little I knew then how much it mattered - the innocence of childhood snatched so deceptively in so many little ways from the life of a very little girl. So untrusting I couldn't close my eyes even for a second for fear my best friends might hurt me. So insecure I thought I would be ridiculed for enjoying the fresh air. So self-loathing I felt I didn't deserve more than a lungful of garbage.

## Chapter Four
### * * *

The end of each school year found my parents yelling at each other in their most belligerent voices. With school over, Mamma would not wait much longer to take Micah and Randy to Granny's house for a week's visit. It made life far easier for her. She got a much needed break from the mental stress she always endured, knowing they were unhappy at home. One thing she did not have to do was worry about us when we stayed with Granny.

Daddy always objected at first with threats and pleas about how much he would miss us. Finally, he would agree to let the boys go, but swore he couldn't endure a week without his little girl. That argument had kept me from going until now. Granny started having a say in the matter on my birthday this year. Ever since, my mother always closed any discussion with Daddy on the subject by saying, "Well, talk to Mamma about it." I never knew what Granny said to him, but whatever it was, she only had to say it once. He never argued with her.

Daddy protested letting me spend my first week away from him by refusing to accompany us on the trip to Alabama. That made us all the happier. It was a long drive to Granny's house, and we three children succumbed to dreamland long before we reached our destination. The car jostled back and forth over the dirt and rock driveway as it climbed the small grade and came to a stop in front of the white frame house.

Granny had been sitting up waiting for us, as was her custom. When she saw the headlights approaching, she met us at the car with flashlight in hand and shined it in front of us all the way to the porch, admonishing us to be careful. There was no indoor bathroom here, so we used a porcelain chamber pot next to the bed if we needed to before we climbed into bed.

The next day Granny helped us fashion sailboats out of plastic butter dishes she had been collecting for that purpose. Mamma looked as though she wanted to stay a week herself instead of going home. I wished she could, too. I wished we could live here and never see Daddy again. Just before she left to go home, Mamma took out a bag and surprised us with plastic pinwheels she had bought for each of us and miraculously had kept hidden from the three plunderers in the car with her. She told Granny it might help keep us out of her hair.

"I ain't worried about that," Granny replied. "If I had to have something to keep my grandbabies out of my hair what would be the use of living?"

"I laid their church clothes out in the back bedroom," Mama said. She was good at jumping from one subject to another with no warning. "And I put a piece of plastic on the bed where Karen will sleep."

We all said our good-byes and watched and waved as Mamma drove away. I was sad for her, and I felt guilty that she had to contend with Daddy all by herself that week. Most likely Mamma was in hog heaven knowing she had a few days to herself.

Granny filled a big tub in the backyard with water and the younger ones entertained themselves sailing their little plastic boats. I felt too big to be having fun in such a frivolous way, so I left my cousins and brothers to their play and followed Granny inside. As she began to prepare lunch, I swept the kitchen with Granny's homemade broom. While I straightened the sheets on Granny's bed I longed to see how fast my pinwheel would turn if I held it in front of the electric fan. Micah had asked to do that when Mamma gave them to us and had been denied his request. Granny was too practical and too poor to use electricity in such a wasteful manner. I was never aware that she played favorites, yet I knew if I asked anything in private most all my wishes would be granted. In this particular incident I never had to ask.

"You are sweatin' up a storm, Katie. Sit here in front of this fan 'fore you have a heat stroke. You needn't kill yourself in this house. We got all day to make those beds," Granny continued as she stooped over to plug the fan into the extension cord. Of course I knew enough to keep these little favors quiet and not flaunt it before my brothers and cousins. And so I sat before the electric fan on that sweltering day holding my plastic pinwheel and dreaming of other lands and other people. It was great to be six years old and have Granny in the next room.

A whole week of pleasure loomed ahead of me. I allowed myself to daydream about the plans we already had for the next few days. Tomorrow we would walk to church and Monday Granny would drive us to town and then... Suddenly, the sound of voices in the kitchen interrupted my reverie. Quickly I turned off the fan, hid the pinwheel, and finished making the bed. It would never do for the adults (or other children for that matter) to see me sitting idle. Better for them to see me working. "Idleness is the devil's workshop." Mamma's words rang in my ears. Maybe if I organized Granny's sewing box, the guilty feeling would go away. Besides, Granny always praised me for being such a good helper.

I skirted through the tiny center hall and peered into the kitchen, not wanting to be seen by whoever was talking to my grandmother. I recognized the man and knew him to be a long time friend of hers. He stood holding his hat in his hands,

41

nervously turning it slowly as he spoke.

"Miz Ginny, I don't believe anyone's got word to you yet that old man Peterson passed on just a little while ago. Miz Peterson asked me to let you know on my way home."

"Hush yo mouth," Granny said softly. That was the colloquial way of saying she couldn't believe it. "What happened to him, Jed?" she asked.

"Doc figures it must have been a heart attack. He was working on that new room they's apputin' on their house and he jest fell over. Didn't make no sound or nothin'."

"Well, I knowed I seen him in town jest yestiddy and he wasn't complainin' about a thang," Granny said as she pulled out a chair from the kitchen table and slowly eased herself into it as though the news were too heavy for her to handle standing up.

"I'll git on the phone and let Miz Hunt and everybody on that end of the road know. We'll have somethin' to eat over there 'fore supper time," she continued. Granny was already setting the wheels in motion for the community to rally around a friend and neighbor in need. I knew from experience the family would not want for anything for the next few days, except maybe privacy.

"I'll pass that on to Miz Peterson, Miz Ginny, and I'll stop by Eddie Howard's place and make sure he knows since he ain't got no phone. Well, I best be goin'. You take care of yoreself now." As he turned to go, he caught sight of me standing in the doorway.

"Well, hello little lady," he said. I looked down at my feet and bit my bottom lip. I wasn't sure if this was one of those times when children should be seen and not heard, or if it would be rude to not speak to the man.

He looked back at my grandmother and said, "Lord, Rose's girl is growing like a weed. She gonna be staying with you all week?"

"Two, if we can talk her Pa and her Ma into it," Granny answered.

This unexpected comment was news to me. I ran to Granny and hugged her around the leg, breaking my silence to beg to call my mother and find out. They both laughed, and the neighbor said I sure got over being shy awful quick. I smiled at him and he didn't look as frightening to me when I met his eyes this time. But then nothing ever looked as frightening when Granny was by my side.

"I thank you for stoppin' by and lettin' us know, Jed," Granny told him.

"Well, the Lord knows what's best. At least he didn't suffer." He tipped his hat to us as he made his departure.

"Granny, why did he die?" I asked.

"Well, Sugar, dying is part of livin'. The good Lord planned it that way. When we finish our work here, we go home to be with Him. If you love Him, dying is not a bad thing."

"Does it hurt to die?" My questioning mind was in unexplored territory.

"No, it hurts while you are still alive. When you die, the good Lord takes all the pain away."

"I wish I could die," I told her in such a matter-of-fact voice that she jerked her head in my direction. Instinctively I knew I had said the wrong thing. I sneaked a peak at my grandmother and wished I could erase my last comment. Her dear old face looked worried and unsure. Suddenly she laughed and said, "In God's time, honey. In God's time."

I wasn't sure what that meant, but death fascinated me from that point on. If it didn't hurt to die and it's not a bad thing and all the pain goes away and God wants us all to die... well then, that means things will get better! I was ecstatic and couldn't wait for my turn. I spent a lot of time wondering about that mysterious sphere between heaven and earth. I dreamed about it, longed for it, and it never once occurred to me to fear it.

"Now I lay me down to sleep
I pray thee, Lord, my soul to keep
If I should die before I wake
I pray Thee, Lord, my soul to take."

My bedtime prayer became my heart's desire that I should not wake with the morning light.

* * * * *

A footpath, defoliated by years of use, connected Granny's back door to Aunt Helen's, some 200 feet away. The path continued to the house on the other side of my aunt's where Robin Granger lived with her mother and stepfather. Robin was eight years older than me, and sometimes she enjoyed spending time with me. I talked to her about dying, and she agreed with me.

Robin said, "It beats the hell out of living." Some folks said Robin was a little rough around the edges to be just fourteen, but she always treated me with gentleness. Robin was somehow related through marriage to my Aunt Hattie who lived on the other side of Granny.

Granny's kitchen was the hub of life in her house, as kitchens were in most of the homes in the area, and Granny never used any other room when guests were present. "Folks just seem to feel more at home in here," she explained.

For this reason the room was a collage of necessary items. The insurance policies hung in their respective pouches outlining the open doorway leading to the back porch. The insurance men came by once a month to collect on the premiums. Granny kept life insurance policies on each of her children and grandchildren, plus health and life policies on herself. The different colored pouches representing the various companies hung ready with the exact amount of cash inside when their day of collection arrived. If for some reason Granny

44

could not be at home when they arrived, the agents understood they should come on in and collect the money and mark it paid for her.

Granny never met a stranger. She considered everyone friends. Mr. Brown from the Farm Bureau or Mr. Smith from Cotton States or any other visitor would fix himself a cup of coffee while she dished him up some blackberry cobbler or cut him a piece of Aunt Hattie's coconut cake.

"Mind you don't get that cup off the top shelf that's got my teeth in it," she would remind the friendly businessmen upon every visit. As if they would forget a thing like that! We all knew that her store bought teeth were in a permanent state of retirement in the cracked brown ceramic cup. She claimed she could gum anything she wanted better than she could chew it with those fake teeth. Once I asked her why she didn't throw them away.

"They cost too durn much money to throw away!" she exclaimed. Granny never threw anything away. She still kept her appendix in a jar of formaldehyde in the back room next to the old calendar with a picture of the Dionne quintuplets across the top.

The pot-bellied, coal burning stove sat in a place of honor near a corner, sending a pungent smoky odor throughout the room on wintry days. Coal was expensive and not to be wasted. Granny let the fire die out each night and relit it each morning before she did anything else. She placed a pan of fresh water on top of the stove every morning, and it sat ready for instant use when needed. Granny said it put moisture back into the air. I just knew we mixed the hot water with some of the frigid tap water in another pan to get some warm enough to bathe our bodies.

The house was built by Granny, Grandaddy, and friends and neighbors. No doubt Granny designed the structure. In keeping with her practical nature, she did not waste one inch of

*45*

space and did not spend one dime on anything more than bare necessities. Granny had opted for as much square footage as she could afford rather than unseen niceties. That included foregoing insulation between the inside and outside walls. The four room structure sat on block pillars and though Granny talked about underpinning it until the year she died, she never made it a priority. Therefore, it was always hotter inside in summer than it was in the yard, and it was colder than outside temperatures in the winter.

The house also included a large front porch which served as a most popular gathering place. Designed to accommodate a lot of people, it was home to several rockers, a straight chair, a porch swing, numerous squirrels and a bullfrog named Pete. Micah was partial to Pete and once tried to sneak him into the car for a trip to town. He learned real quick that Granny was not in favor of domesticating wild animals.

Going to town with Granny was an event. She would settle her small frame behind the wheel of her 1934 Ford, and we all took our places beside and behind her. We looked forward to helping her drive. Truth is, she probably could not have made it to town without us. She made a ceremony out of putting on her wire-rim glasses. Granny rarely got in a hurry, and this was certainly never one of those times.

"Hand me my pocketbook, somebody," she would say. Granny's life was an open book. The doors to her house were never locked. She shared her food, her phone, her feelings with anyone who came along, but her pocketbook was her private domain. She allowed no one to get the glasses out for her. We passed the purse and waited somewhat impatiently while she found her glasses and fitted them on her face.

"I'm getting to where I cain't see a thang without my glasses," she complained. "And I cain't see too good with 'em either. You boys cut that out back there," she directed toward the back seat. "If'n you're figurin' on roughhousin' all the way to town, you'll have me nervous as a cat. Turn around and help me get out on the road."

Our job was to look behind and ahead of us and tell her when a car was approaching. When we saw one coming, Granny would pull off the road if she could, so we would not be in the way. If another car came up behind us and she couldn't pull off the road, she would slow to a crawl and we would all stick our arms out the window and motion the other driver to go around us.

"If you young'uns see anything comin' in from the side, holler. I ain't never run into anybody and I don't aim to start now." Everyone who lived anywhere near her street knew Miss Ginny's driving style and made allowances for it. They sometimes teased her about it and offered to get whatever she needed from the store for her, so she wouldn't have to drive. Anyone who knew her at all, however, knew her well enough to know Miss Ginny did not give up anything until she had to. She good-naturedly assured more than one well-intentioned neighbor, "When I get too old or too addle-brained to take care of business, I'll let you know." Taking care of business referred to paying her bills in person.

My favorite part of going to town was going in to pay the electric, phone, or water bill while Granny waited in the closest available parking place with the younger kids. It must have been Granny's favorite part of going to town, too. She took advantage of those few minutes under the shade of the big oak trees that lined the street to have a dip of Bruton's sweet snuff. When asked why she dipped snuff, she said, "It's a nasty habit. Don't ever start it. Same thang goes for cigarettes. Them thangs will kill you."

"Which is worse, Granny?" I asked. Life for me was a series of comparisons.

"Well, they're both bad habits. Won't neither of them send you to the devil, but they both make you smell like you've been there," she said.

"Then why do you do it?" I asked with timidity and some degree of trepidation. It wasn't a wise idea to question an adult. Even my patient and loving grandmother might not take too kindly to a prying child. I underestimated her, as usual. She seemed anxious to explain.

"I didn't know no better when I started it," she said. "I thought I could try it a few times and see what it was like. Then before I knew it, I couldn't quit 'cause my body craved it so bad. I'd cut off my right arm if I could give it up, and I'd cut off both my arms if it would make any difference in keeping my grandyounguns from getting hooked on any of that mess. Cigars, chewing tobacco; it's all the same."

I had a mental picture of Granny standing with both arms missing and blood pouring out from her shoulders. It must be powerful stuff, I thought. Granny could do anything she wanted to do. If any substance was more powerful than Granny, I didn't want any part of it. I made a determination then and there that no cigarette or alcohol would ever pass my lips.

"Folks just wasn't educated on such things back then," she continued. "I want you younguns to get all the schoolin' you kin but remember not all learnin' takes place in the school house. You kin learn your best lessons from others' mistakes. I hope this is one you don't ever make."

"You don't have to worry about me, Granny!" I assured her. Much as I loved my granny and wanted to be just like her, I didn't want to have to carry a spit can everywhere I went!

The oppressingly hot day made me bored and restless. "I can't wait for school to start," I said. (Granny had just brought to mind one of my favorite things.) "And I'll be glad when it's winter. It's too hot!"

"Aw! Quit wishin' your life away! Cold weather will be here before you know it, Katie, and then you'll wish it was summertime. Make the most you kin of today."

She was right. The winter of my seventh year seemed especially harsh. Perhaps it wasn't. Perhaps it only felt more severe, in the same sense that all of life seemed more severe. It was embarrassing to be poor. People should never have to be poor in winter. It is a double mockery of human dignity. I hated wearing cardboard cutouts of the outline of my foot inside my shoes and stuffing toilet paper into the toes because the closest thing the shoe store's clearance table had was far too big for my feet. My mother's philosophy was "If it's cheap, buy it. If it doesn't fit your body, make your body fit it."

I knew people knew. Of course they had to know. Somehow they were able to see with X-ray vision through the outer surface of the shoe into the toilet paper crammed at the end of my toes. They could tell there was a hole growing steadily bigger in the cardboard where my big toe kept rubbing, rubbing until the cardboard wore down into long skinny rolls like so many little pinworms.

To make matters worse, my feet had chosen this year to outgrow or outwear all my socks. Mamma said there was no money for socks, so I was given the choice of using a pair of Micah's or doing without. Wear boys' socks with my dresses? People looked at me funny enough already. No thanks. I would go without. Maybe no one would say anything. Usually kids were very polite to me because they liked me, but wearing boys' socks would be an open invitation for ridicule.

I resented having to walk to school anyway. My mother was home, and she had a car. Everyone else rode to school on days like this, but Mamma didn't want to take Randy out in the cold weather. That was just an excuse, I thought. She didn't let the cold weather stop her if it were something she wanted to do.

I walked along in resentful daydreams and thus did not hear the car pull up beside me. The driver had to ask me twice if I wanted a ride.

"No... thank you," I said through chattering teeth.

"Are you sure, honey? You're awfully cold," the nice female voice asked. "My daughter Susie is in your class. I'd like to take you to school."

"I can't," I replied, shivering even more now that fright was added to the cold weather. The car wasn't even headed toward the school. It was going in the opposite direction. I shook my head and started walking again. I hoped she would turn around and follow me. Next time someone offers me a ride, I'm going with them. And maybe they will kidnap me and then my mother will be sorry, I thought.

Three blocks did not seem far to walk in the spring or fall, but every step of the way tortured my body in the bitter morning chill. The icy wind whipped at my flimsy dress, wrapping the skirt part around my stiff, barely movable legs.

I welcomed the sight of the school building, and reviving heat met me at the door. Instantly, pain crept into my feet and toes, forcing me to hobble past the students lined against the wall by classes, past the watchful eyes of teachers into the privacy of the girls' bathroom. I removed my shoes and sat on the toilet seat holding my toes in my hand. I thought I would surely cry out, so great was the unexpected pain.

The sun lent its penetrating warmth to the earth during the day, lessening the avenging cold that threatened frostbite earlier. The walk home was so much more tolerable that I marveled at the morning's pain.

I was scarcely in the house before someone knocked on our front door. My mother, always curious and always ready to visit, hastened to answer it.

"Mrs. Carter, I'm Susie Taylor's mother. She and Karen are in the same class at school. I passed Karen walking to school today and offered her a ride. She was afraid to get in the car with me, so she walked, but I couldn't help but notice she was not wearing any socks." She held up her hand as if to stop my mother before she could say anything. "Now, I know how kids are, and she's probably got a drawer full of socks and just forgot to put any on, but it did remind me that I have two bags of Susie's clothes from last year that I have to get rid of. I'd be delighted if you would let Karen go through them and see if there is anything she can wear. Some of it is just about new and they ought to fit Karen perfectly."

My mother received the offer with gratefulness. She had never been known to turn down a free offer. She invited Mrs. Taylor in and they talked about neighborly things. I wished she would hurry and leave and come back with the promised goods. I was so excited!

I thought how smoothly Mrs. Taylor had worded what she wanted to say. How tactful, and to the point and... friendly. She brought the clothes to my house that night as she promised. I never had much contact with her after that, just as I never had much with her before, but I thought of her and Susie every time I pulled on warm knee socks in the freezing weather. I revelled in their fuzzy softness, thrilled to have colors to match my dresses.

* * * * *

My mother was acting weird toward me lately. I thought maybe Daddy being laid off until Lockheed got another contract caused her strange behavior. She worked all the time to make up for his loss of salary, and she always yelled at him for drinking up the money she made. I blamed him for her discontent with me, regardless of whether he was responsible. Mamma would fight with Daddy and then look at me as if she didn't know who I was. And I never knew what to expect from her. I thought she would be mad because I had upset Mrs. Taylor, but she hugged me and said I was very smart not to get in the car with someone without permission.

At other times she would find me and stand with a belt in

51

her hand, demanding, "Do you want your spanking now or after supper?" Stupid question!

"After supper," I always answered, never knowing why she wanted to spank me. Only once did she remember or still desire to spank me after supper.

"Why did you do that?" I asked between whimpers.

"How dare you pretend you don't know!" she glared down at me, fire emanating from her eyes. "And don't you ever, EVER do it again."

So I determined not to ever, ever do again whatever it was I had done.

"You sit there and think about it until you figure it out," she shouted at me. It was too confusing. It was too unfair! No one could make me think, after all! I could just sit and be blank and then I couldn't be wrong because I wouldn't be anything. I would concentrate on not concentrating, and then for a while, I would fall asleep.

Maybe she was only acting this way because she was expecting. I hoped she wouldn't be so mean after the baby came out.

Predictably, the harshness of winter gave way to spring, and the early days of summer brought a new life to share the miseries of our home. Mamma named him Jeffrey Scott, and she said there would be no more babies. She wrapped him in tenderness and treated him forever after as her baby.

My mother hated me. I hated me too. Sometimes I could not remember which classroom I belonged in or my teacher's name. Sometimes I walked right past my house and then could not remember where it was. It was hard to gauge the time of day, and I could never remember if I had eaten anything since I woke up.

My mother would start a sentence, then look at me as if she wanted me to finish it for her. Finally, one day she said to me, "I'm only going to ask you this once and I'm not ever going to ask you again. Has your Daddy ever touched you where he shouldn't?" Hostility weighted her words, and her question caught me by surprise. We weren't supposed to talk about this. Daddy said so. I looked down at the floor, unable to answer.

"Answer me Karen, and look me in the eye when you do. I want the truth!" Anger saturated her voice.

I wanted to tell her. Oh, how I wanted her to make it all stop. Embarrassed, I looked into her face and the message was clear. "Lie to me!" it begged. "I don't want to have to know for sure. Don't drag me into your problem. I have enough of my own."

Her face was livid. What would happen if I said yes? She was not holding a belt, but would she beat me anyway? Would she blame me? Of course she would blame me. Mamma always said if a woman let herself get raped it was her own fault. She either dressed wrong or she wore perfume or she shouldn't have been in that place at that time. It didn't matter what she may have been doing, it had to be her fault because men had biological urges and couldn't help themselves. It was the woman's responsibility to see to it the man was not aroused. If he became aroused to the point of taking advantage of her, she must have done something to encourage him.

Daddy did tell me he couldn't help himself because I looked so cute in my new dress and shoes, or my hair smelled so nice and clean, he just had to bury himself in it. I tried to stay away from Daddy when I had just washed my hair and tried to not wear things he said he liked. Still, she would say it was my fault.

"Has your daddy ever touched you?" she repeated, emphasizing each word.

"No," I answered softly.

"Good. I didn't think so, but someone told me he did and I had to find out. I don't want this mentioned again," she said as she turned and left the room.

53

I wasn't going to bring it up! Who would I tell? Certainly not her. Alone again, I stood mute with a new humiliation. Someone knew! Who was it? Maybe they didn't really know. Maybe they only thought they knew. It didn't matter if they really knew or not. Someone, somewhere visualized me in that condition. I felt raped all over again, stripped of any dignity or privacy. How would I ever face anyone again? I suspected every person I knew of being the one who told Mamma. It couldn't be my brother, or could it? Mrs. Wilson? She couldn't possibly know. But school teachers knew everything. Did that include... this? What about Mrs. Jones? My Sunday School teacher? Granny? The doctor?

Was this more evidence that it was wrong? Mamma seemed to agree with Daddy that it should not be talked about. But she also acted like I should not let Daddy do it. If it was wrong, why would the preacher say to do everything our parents tell us to do? Could I trust anyone to tell me the truth?

I had been seven years old when my baby brother was born in May. I felt responsible for him, and I loved pretending I was his Mommy, dressing him in my little doll dresses. In my pretend world he was a baby girl, but I never wished he was a girl in real life. I thought it safer for him to be a boy, and I loved him very much. I was glad my only sister had died at birth. I wanted a sister in the worst way, but I rejoiced for her that she did not have to live in this family. I knew heaven offered her more happiness. I did not remember her since I was only 21 months old at the time she was born. She died during the birth process because no doctor was attending my mother. He was out to lunch, probably in more ways than one, I thought. The autopsy showed the baby had drowned. She was lucky, I thought. If God could take new babies back to heaven, why wouldn't He take me? I must not be good enough.

I came home from school one fall day to find Mamma talking to another lady. Mamma's agitation rose as she told the lady how much she loved her children and how much she sacrificed for us.

"I am concerned about the lack of supervision," the woman explained. "Who watches them while you work?"

"Go on to the bedroom. We're talking," my mother said to me.

The jagged edge of fear jabbed at my throat. I had heard of the welfare department who had the power to take children away and split them up into different foster homes. I wondered if the lady came from there, and if she had found out about last Halloween.

Mamma had left Jeff alone, asleep in his crib, while she worked at the fall festival at our school. She told us to go trick-or-treating and to not worry about Jeff. We did go trick-or-treating, but I could not stop thinking about my baby brother. What if someone stole him when no one was home? What if the house caught on fire again like it did the year before? I left my friends and older brother to go home and stay with Jeff. She probably knew I would. She had taken Randy with her to the school carnival, but she saw no harm in leaving six-month-old Jeff asleep in his crib.

I looked from the lady to my mother. I picked Jeff up and took him into the bedroom to play.

"Please don't think I'm here to interfere," I heard the lady say as I left the room. "I'm here to offer advice or help you if I can. Let's talk about the children."

Jeff was wet, so I changed his diaper, robot-like, not speaking, not smiling, just doing what needed to be done. I needed a pencil to do my homework. We kept them in a desk drawer in the dining room. Before I reached the desk, I heard Mamma speaking my name. I leaned hard against the wall and listened.

"I don't know if I should be worried about Karen or not," Mamma was saying.

"What concerns you about her?"

"She's just real quiet. She don't ever talk anymore if she don't have to."

"How old is she?" the lady asked.

"She was seven in January," my mother answered.

"Seven is a hard age. She'll probably outgrow whatever is upsetting her." Profound advice from yet another adult who didn't know enough or care enough to get involved.

Whatever bothered me bothered me more as time wore on. Bothered me so much that the year became a blur in my memory, and something dreadful was forced to hide in the dungeon of my mind, so that I could still function in my life.

Seven: Second grade. Old teacher, strict and pious. Morning devotions going on too long. Raised hand desperately asking permission to be excused. Hot liquid running down my leg.

Seven: A new brother born in the spring. Daddy says Mamma won't sleep with him anymore. My job now.

Seven: Migraine headaches. Abscessed teeth. Novocaine that didn't work. Dr. Frost. Stupid name. Stupid dentist. Legs hurting incredibly bad. Mamma says it is growing pains, not to worry about them.

Seven: Sound asleep - wide awake. Man in my room looking down at me in the dark. Moonlight behind his silhouette. My body frozen in place. Eyes wide with terror. Can't move. Can't breathe. Daddy. I should have known.

Seven: No more visits to Dr. Weaver. Something horrible is happening, but I don't know what. Can't look in mirrors. Must never see myself again. The lake, Daddy's friends. What was it about Daddy and his friends?

Seven: Fingers over my lips, fist over my mouth - nervous habits, both. Tongue hurts. I won't talk. I promise.

Yeah, "seven is a hard age."

# Chapter Five

### * * *

The old folks looked forward to our family reunions like children looked for Christmas. I loved it when the reunion was held at Granny's house, because I could be in on all the preparations. The wooden stools and ladder-back chairs were retrieved from the shed behind the house to be cleaned up and repaired if necessary. Several makeshift tables had to be constructed under the big oak tree in the front yard or under the pecan trees behind the house. Soon to be heavy-laden with foods of all description, (and some beyond description, I always thought), these tables needed to be strong and sturdy. The night before the big day, Granny let me plunder through the linen drawer and choose enough tablecloths to cover the outside tables. It did not matter that stains and raveled edges adorned most of the old cotton and linen relics. I loved the feel and motley assortment of designs woven into them. You would have thought the Queen of England was expected for dinner, the way I poured over them before making final selections.

Relatives from all parts of Florida, Alabama, and Georgia began arriving on Saturday. A very few would stay in a motel or with other people they knew in the area, but most staked their claim to beds and floor space in Granny's and Aunt Helen's houses. Those who lived close enough to make it a one day trip would usually wait until the big day and arrive as early as possible to get the most from their visit.

The joy in Mamma's and Granny's faces increased with each arriving car. I was not so much thrilled over all the people who came from far away as I was excited over having a big party with the more familiar faces. I hung around Aunt Helen, carrying one of her two little girls on my hip whenever possible. I stuck close to Robin or Aunt Hattie, Mamma, or Granny. I thought it fun to be on the edge of the excitement but too scary to be in the middle of it all.

I, too, could hardly wait for our reunions. In fact, the only bad thing about family reunions was my immediate family. Micah never missed a chance to torment me and he saw no reason to clean up his act for company. The summer of 1958 was no exception. The day was still and nauseously hot, as south Alabama is prone to be in July. As I sat under the shade of the pecan tree surrounded by kin I did not know, my father emerged from the storage shed so drunk he could hardly stand. At the sight of him, having already been in a nervous state, I had a sudden, uncontrollable urge to pee. I ran for the back door, hoping no one would be in the newly added bathroom.

As it turned out, waiting for someone to come out of the bathroom would have been less of a problem than the one I encountered. My brother came out of the back door as I started to go in, and he began to sway from one side of the doorway to the other, preventing me from entering.

"Fatty, fatty, two-by-four, can't get through the back porch door!" he chanted, sticking his tongue out as far as possible and making ape faces in between chants. Temporarily distracted from my mission, I glared at the wagging offensive muscle and wondered if everyone's tongue was that ugly when that much exposed.

Micah stood in the doorway, blocking my path by spreading both arms and legs to cover the opening. I begged and whined until hot tears of frustration welled up making two pools of anger where my eyes belonged. Suddenly Micah stepped back against the door frame to make room for a boy coming out of the house to pass him. With only one foot in the yard and the other still in the doorway, the boy turned to face Micah and said to him, "Why don't you find a boy your size to pick on and leave her alone?"

Micah didn't answer, but after meeting the other boy's eyes for a few seconds, he scooted into the back yard and lost himself in the crowd of relatives.

"Go on in," the boy said, motioning for me to pass him. I took my red face and the remainder of my pride inside. It wouldn't do for me to stop at the bathroom now. He would see me go in there for sure, and I was embarrassed enough already. I walked into the kitchen and, for lack of any other place to go, right on out the front door.

To my great relief, I saw Robin on the front porch leaning against the brick column and talking to two other big people I did not know. I stood beside her until the others finished talking and excused themselves to take their places in line around the overladen tables. Only then did I notice the boy from the back porch had made his way into the front yard.

I tugged at Robin's blouse, hoping to get her attention without attracting anyone else's. "Who's that boy?" I asked, pointing to his back.

"That's Joyce and Bill's boy," she said. "His name is Brad."

Brad. Hmmm. He had piqued my curiosity. Ten-year-old boys weren't usually nice to girls. Yet he had been nice to me. I watched him with interest out of the corner of my eye, not with suspicion, just curiosity.

Everyone seemed to be outside finding something to eat. In the privacy of the moment, I slipped away to use the bathroom. When that order of business was accomplished, I returned to the porch and looked around to find someone I knew. While I surveyed the scene before me, a man came around the corner of the house and spoke to a group of men standing below me at the foot of the steps.

"Johnny, bring one of those men with strong muscles with you and come around back. Lester's fallen out of the chair and we can't get him up."

"Is he hurt?" Johnny asked as he and two other men followed Uncle Bill.

"No. He's just had too much to drink. He'd be better off if we can get him inside to bed."

He's so stupid, I thought, mortified. Can't he quit drinking for just one day? Why does he have to make a fool of himself when all the family is here? I didn't want anyone to know I was his daughter. I slipped away alone to Helen and Johnny's house walking as fast as I could through the uncut area of grass and weeds to reach their front porch. No one used that entrance and, as I had thought, it was deserted and quiet there. Only the sound of my heavy, angry breathing broke the silence as I sat on the step and scratched a furious itch that consumed my bare feet.

"Don't scratch that!" a familiar voice commanded. Robin appeared instantly beside me, inspecting my feet as she spoke. "I was looking for you," she said. "Did you step in an ant bed?"

"I don't know," I wailed as my feet continued to torment me.

"I don't see any bites or rash," Robin said, lifting my foot to see it better in the sunlight.

"Stinging nettles. That's what it is. Be still! I'll be right back," she called as she ran to find something to help her remove the nettles. Carefully she pulled out the nearly invisible hairs that transferred from the plant into my skin while I struggled to refrain from rubbing them in further. Then she showed me some stinging nettle plants so I would know what it was I shouldn't step on again.

"Aunt Ginny is setting out the cinnamon rolls you wanted

and all the rest of the desserts. Let's go get some before they're all gone," she suggested brightly.

"I don't want any," I said. "Anyway, I'm not going back down there as long as my daddy is there."

"Well, I'm going to go get something for myself and I'll bring something back for you," she said.

While she was gone I thought about what I wanted to say to my mother. It's all her fault, I thought. I knew she was just as embarrassed as I, but we wouldn't be embarrassed if she would quit letting him come with us to the reunions.

"Why don't you leave him?" I demanded of my mother afterwards. He makes me sick!"

"Don't talk about your Daddy like that. He's the one that's sick. His drinking is a sickness and I promised to stay by him in sickness and in health. I'm not going to leave him when he needs me."

"If he's sick, he should go to a doctor!" I retaliated.

"He can't help himself, Karen. He came into this world craving the stuff. His mamma laid up drunk all the time and she fed it to him when he was just a baby. All of his brothers drank and he just never knew any better."

I didn't want to hear it, all her excuses for his rank behavior. "Why do you always tell him you're going to leave him and then you never do?" It was a fair accusation in question form. I didn't receive an answer.

My father was the youngest of twelve children, all boys except the oldest. His only sister served as more of a mother to him. Grandma Carter was a white-haired, snuff-dipping, sickly old lady who rarely left her bed. She slept in a fourposter bed in her front room which reeked of whisky and urine. I detested having to kiss her fat, flabby face almost as much as she detested children. With over twenty grandchildren before us, we weren't exactly good news when we came along. Still, I thought it very rude of her to grunt and say, "How many does that make you now, Lester?" when we went to visit soon after Jeff's birth.

I cared for very few people on my father's side of the family. His older sister, Aunt Lucy, lived in Phenix City, and we saw her every time we took a trip to Granny's house. She was okay except she thought anything her youngest brother did was all right. The best thing about Aunt Lucy's house was the Coke machine. Her son-in-law had managed to obtain the contraption when all the businesses in the area purchased new ones and phased out the old models.

Aunt Lucy knew the way to a child's heart. She kept a supply of dimes to put in the palm of our hands and allowed us to get our own Cokes from the outdated machine.

Mamma always protested letting me have one, but Aunt Lucy usually won the argument to let me have one like the rest of the kids. Daddy never opposed anything his big sister said, so I suppose Mamma felt a losing battle coming on and did not put up much of a fight.

The bottled Cokes were factory fresh, unopened and icy cold. Although it was only with his permission that I was allowed to have one, I still felt a sense of triumph to parade past my father, taking not only the first and last swallow myself, but all those in-between. This drink belonged to me, untainted by his foul body. Furthermore, I didn't have to share it with any of my brothers like Mamma made us do. When she had her way, I took one sip, then each of my brothers took a sip, taking turns until it was all gone. Randy and Jeff both put the whole bottle top in their mouths when they drank. Micah drank the correct way, but he could "sip" two ounces in one swallow! Mamma was right. I preferred clean, unused drinks and if I couldn't have it that way, I didn't want any at all. I was getting that way about a lot of things. I didn't demand the best, but I wanted what I wanted. I didn't compromise well.

Granny lived thirty miles from the back gate of Fort

Benning Army Base, a fact that made little difference to me as a child. It was, however, the subject of many of her true life stories she was fond of telling. I never once heard her speak ill of a soldier. She held them collectively in high esteem and she claimed that "some of 'em might get a little rowdy ev'ry now and then, but I ain't never had no trouble out of ere one of 'em". She always said if we could trust them to protect us overseas, she thought she could trust them in her own yard.

Granny didn't often relate her own personal tragedies, but most folks who knew her well knew that her firstborn, a daughter, had died while temporarily being looked after by a soldier. He was renting a room from them at the time while he recovered from a broken leg. Granny ran a boarding house, and she cooked and served breakfast for the tenants. On that particular morning the infant, only six weeks old, was still sleeping in the room next to the soldier when Granny went downstairs to fix the morning meal. Granny asked him to listen for the baby and tap on the floor with his cane to let her know when she awoke. He never did. When Granny came upstairs to check on her later, she found the baby still and lifeless. Sometime between Granny's gentle kiss on the child's sleeping cheek and her return an hour or so later, baby Louise slipped away from her, silently and without warning.

From the moment I heard that story, I thought the soldier killed the baby, but Granny was just as sure he didn't. Naturally I would distrust him. I knew how my father treated my baby brothers, and I always feared they would die from something he did.

For the first time, I privately questioned Granny's judgment. Aloud, I asked how the baby died, what the doctor said about it, how she knew the soldier didn't do anything to her, and a thousand other questions. As I grew older, I learned that Granny didn't have blind trust in anyone, especially where her children were concerned, but neither did she suspect anyone without just cause. I believe she was the most fair person I ever knew. She possessed the unique ability to look at the intent behind someone's behavior, and not just see the results. She sought to understand people without making excuses for them.

I learned early that she accepted me no matter what I did, but I understood just as clearly that she would not cover my tracks if I got into trouble. I heard her say more than once (usually it was to my delinquent older brother), "If you do your best and you make a mistake, I'll help you all I can, but if you do something you know you ain't supposed to do, you are on yore own. Don't come crying to me if you get caught trying to get away with something."

I could sit for hours on the top step of her front porch with my elbows on my knees and my chin in my hands. I did my best thinking there, especially when Granny sat in the porch rocker embroidering pillow cases or pillow "slips" as she called them. We would sit in silence for a long time before Granny invariably asked, "What you thinking about so hard, Katie?"

Oh, the things I thought during those lazy times. Clouds floating overhead became whatever my imagination wanted them to be. If the sky was streaked with pink, I envisioned God making new babies to send down to earth. If more pink than blue colored the heavens, then He was making more girl babies today. If there was more blue than pink... well, maybe God would correct His mistake tomorrow. I always thought boys were more trouble than girls, and I hoped I would never have any. I wasn't quite sure what useful purpose they served, but Robin said it was so they could fight the wars and women didn't have to. I thought that if the world only contained women, there wouldn't be any wars. She really got a kick out of that, and she said I should be President some day, because I had all the right ideas.

Sometimes I sat on Granny's porch and watched the cars

go by. Most of the drivers who traveled the old farm road in front of the house blew their horns, and Granny would lay her embroidery in her lap and wave as they passed. She guessed the destination of each passing vehicle if she didn't already know it for sure. "Well, I see Agnes is going to the doctor. She goes once a week now that her heart started actin' up." Or it might be, "There goes Mary Sims and her brood. She said she had to get them set for school this week. They must be headed for town."

Often as not the passersby would stop and inquire if Miss Ginny needed anything from town or drop off some tomatoes or a mess of green beans they brought her from their garden. Granny always said she was short on a right many things, but good neighbors wasn't one of them. I had to agree with her, except my definition of "neighbor" was someone who lived in the same block. Here, neighbors might live four miles away.

From these lazy, truly carefree days, I gleaned a foundation that anchored me to sanity while growing up in an insane environment. My cousins who lived next door to Granny thought I could walk on water, and I loved being with them. There was always a baby to hold, and that was all I wanted out of life at the tender age of eight.

Granny and Langston (I could never refer to him as Grandaddy since he died when I was a baby and I never really knew him) had donated two acres of land on the back side of their twenty acres for the purpose of building a church. Originally only one room, the first structure was not much more than a place to come in out of the cold. The men of the congregation added a nursery and three rooms for children's classes to the front side of the sanctuary, but membership soon grew from the small nucleus of believers to encompass a larger number of the growing community.

I sat on the edge of Granny's property and watched with my brothers and cousins through the trees as construction workers erected a new church building and cleared and graveled a parking area. The new, modern gathering place had real heat. Though it lacked modern air conditioning, we did have an adequate number of hand held paper fans supplied by the local funeral home.

Sunday School at Granny's resembled Sunday School at my church, except the teachers went out of their way to make me feel at home, because I was visiting. I looked forward to today's lesson. The teacher said last week we would be talking about parents today. She said they are also accountable to God for the things they do and that sometimes they do wrong, too. The teacher opened the lesson with prayer and then began, "It is most important to our Heavenly Father that we listen to and obey our earthly parents. He gave us parents for a reason. Did you know he gave your Mom and Dad a job to do? Their job is to teach you to love God. Your job is to obey them and learn from them."

"What if they tell you to do something and you think you shouldn't do it?" a boy in the back row asked. I jerked my head around to see who was bold enough to ask what I was thinking. I studied his face. He seemed honest and sincere, not smart alecky as I first thought. I recognized him and knew his Mom taught the children's choir and his Dad taught the boys' missionary study group.

No doubt our teacher kept that in mind when she replied, "It is often difficult to know what is wrong and what is right. We all have times when we really don't want to do something that is required of us. But we grow into better people when we do it anyway without complaining. Our parents know what is best for us and they want what is best for us, so we should obey them without questioning their authority."

My eyes filled with tears and I bowed my head so no one would notice. Everywhere I turned someone was telling me that Daddy was right and I was wrong. It wasn't fair! It just wasn't fair!

In Sunday School we sang, "Jesus loves me this I know for the Bible tells me so." Normally little children ask no more than that assurance because love is all they are looking for. I, of course, needed to know what else the Bible said. It did not impress me that Jesus loved me because I had the wrong connotation of love.

People frequently said I was the apple of my daddy's eye. Daddy assured me he loved me. Love meant sex because that's when he loved me the most. Over and over he assured me all daddies loved their little girls and did the same things with them. He told me all girls like it and if I didn't then I must not be right with God and therefore wasn't in the right frame of mind for "love". He reminded me that the preacher said we should do what our parents tell us to do because we love them. The Bible did say, "Children, obey your parents". Mamma always said, "Do what your daddy tells you to do." Logic told me, "God is my heavenly father and He says to obey my daddy. God gave us parents to teach us about Him. So this must be something God requires me to do. After all, Scripture supports it." But my heart wrenched itself inside out screaming all the way, "NO! I can't do this anymore!"

When I was with my father I did what he required me to do. During some episodes I threw up or I cried or I became angry. Of course I had to suppress that anger so he would not become angry. But every time I pretended it was happening to the other *me* and when it was over *I* could be myself again. Each time my fear and hatred for him became more intense, and my anger and distrust deepened until around the age of nine I could no longer accept the abuse.

Desperately, I searched the Scriptures for something that would condemn my father's behavior. Only once did I find any support there. "Fathers, provoke not your children to wrath," it said. There was my ammunition! At the next opportunity, I fired that one at my God-fearing mother, knowing she couldn't argue with it. Any one could see he had provoked us to wrath, and clearly that was wrong. God said so.

I learned never to argue with a religious fanatic. They have more scripture up their sleeves than a yard dog has fleas. Mamma promptly recited the one about the husband being the head of the house, and all of us being under submission to him. That would work real well if he were a godly man, I thought. I was just getting to an age where I was assertive enough to tell her that. I also said I didn't think God wanted us to be beat up and sad all the time. She had a chapter and verse for that too. "You're supposed to stay with the unsaved one in hopes he will come to know the Lord," she said.

I didn't have a verse to refute that one. Once again I was defeated. I couldn't argue with her. She gave me a lecture on responsibility. Feelings didn't matter, indeed were not even acknowledged in our household. Once I ventured to express my opinion on someone who was not at the top of my list of favorite people at that time. With all the emotion I could muster I shouted, "I hate her!"

My mother hastened to assure me, "You don't hate anyone. You might dislike her but you don't hate anybody." I was convinced I hated this person, but my mother said I couldn't hate, so I felt guilty and chastised and tried hard never to hate anyone again. My feelings of hatred were forced underground with my feelings of anger only to surface later in life in more inappropriate ways than verbally expressing them.

If I didn't hate, then what was this noxious feeling I had when my father asked, "Do you wear these yet?" holding a box of my mother's sanitary pads in front of me. I blushed scarlet which brought a big, sadistic smile from him. When I told him no, he said, "You let me know when you start wearing them, you hear?" I was still blushing crimson. I could feel it. My face became dry and hot, as if I were standing too close to a fire.

My eyes darted around looking for an escape route, while my mind raced to find an indisputable reason to leave the room.

Some of the older girls at school were talking about those products on the playground, but I had only the vaguest idea of what they were used for. No one had ever explained the facts of life to me, nor would they ever. I only knew this was dirty talk, and Mamma would be mad if I let Daddy talk that way. He had told me on several occasions that when I started wearing those pads, we would be getting a new baby in the family. I knew my mother didn't want to have any more babies, so for her sake, I determined never to let him know when I started having my periods.

Blissfully ignorant of his intentions, the most I experienced from his promise to give me a baby was extreme embarrassment. I was spared the terror and worry he could have inflicted because I lacked the mental maturity to understand his threats. Never verbally graphic, it almost seemed as if Daddy were embarrassed to talk about sex, but he made many subtle references to his plans. Didn't hate? Yes, I did. I hated the way he acted. I hated the way he made me feel. I hated *him*. I hated myself more.

I had heard all my young life that God loved me and sent his Son to die for me to save me from my sins, and that I could live in heaven forever if I accepted Christ as my Savior and let Him tell me what to do with my life. Somehow that was not reassuring, but rather frightening. I considered becoming saved and baptized, but I did not want to go to heaven. I didn't mind dying and would gladly have volunteered for that, if I could die and be done with it. Hell was indescribably bad, and without accepting Jesus I would go there.

I felt certain if God loved me so much and thought I was so special, surely that meant I would be required to have sex with Him when I got to heaven. If sex was so awful with my earthly father, it must be unbearable with God himself. Mamma always talked about how powerful and full of vengeance God is. Being a Christian required loving God, and I just could not do that.

Still too young to understand, I needed to believe God saw my misery and hated it. As I cried myself to sleep night after night, I begged God to make it stop. I developed quite an imagination to help him find a solution. I daydreamed about discovering I was adopted. My birth parents would come and take me away from these horrible people. My "real" parents were wonderful and loved me and after they took me back, I would be so happy that the memory of this miserable life would soon be forgotten. I determined that when I grew up I would have my own orphanage, and I would take care of lots of children, and I wouldn't let anyone hurt them or make them afraid.

In my second favorite daydream (and a more realistic one), my father died and my mother changed. She was not really a bad person, but simply living under too much pressure with my father alive. Maybe neighbors would get nosy and call the police, and they would put him in jail forever. I envied Joseph in the Bible whose brothers sold him into slavery. It seemed like a step up to me!

I purposely put myself in situations where I could be kidnapped or harmed in other ways. I knew better than to ride my bike in the street or to stay out after dark or play alone in deserted places, but they all attracted me like a magnet. No one ever knew if we were tucked into our beds at night, or if we were roaming the streets. It seemed once they told me to do something for my own safety, they left me on my own to do it.

One spring day at the age of nine, I sought solitude in our backyard. I stretched out on the grass and gazed at the cloud formations as they drifted by. The beauty of the heavens mesmerized me, and I thought about life and death as I lay still and quiet. During those moments, God spoke to me, and my soul wrestled with His spirit. I wanted to be left alone, and I did not want to make a commitment to something I did not fully understand. Just as surely as God gives peace that passes understanding, He also burdens a heart beyond endurance. Finally I quit arguing and promised to accept Him and try to do my best for Him from then on.

Words cannot describe the peace and joy that filled my heart. For days I floated around wanting to tell someone the good news. I did not know how to explain. My vocabulary didn't include feeling words. I did tell Mrs. Jones I had been saved, but I could not elaborate when she asked what being saved meant. Of course she already knew, being the daughter of a Methodist minister. She only asked because she wanted to be sure I understood. The following Sunday I walked down the aisle of our church and told the preacher I wanted to be baptized.

I knew that was going to be the most difficult task I had ever voluntarily undertaken. Water terrified me so much that even taking a bath or washing my hair was a frightening ordeal. Oh, why did we have to be Baptists? Janet went to a Methodist church, as did Teresa's family. One house over in either direction and I could have been Methodist! They baptized a different way there. A little water sprinkled over my head didn't sound nearly as scary. I asked Mamma if I could be baptized at one of their churches and Hurricane Rose formed before my very eyes. Not be baptized in the Baptist Church? This family had always been Baptist or nothing at all. Unthinkable heresy!

And so I found myself a week later dressed in a snow white robe descending the steps into the baptismal pool of Gethsemane Heights Baptist Church. And I had asked for this! A man (never mind that he was the preacher) was going to hold a handkerchief over my nose and mouth so I couldn't breathe and push me backwards until I was completely under water in front of hundreds of people. When water filled my ears and the cold wetness cradled the back of my head, I closed my eyes and did what I had always been taught to do. I prayed for deliverance.

# Chapter Six
## * * *

Our Louisiana vacations provided a wonderful break in the monotony of life. Two of Daddy's brothers lived near each other, and they each had two sons and two daughters. We usually stayed at Uncle Lee and Aunt Emma's house. All their children were nice, but I especially liked the girls. Mary Kate was several years older than I, and her sister, Abbie, was a few years younger. Despite the age difference, there were still lots of things we could do together.

Being a city girl, I was thrilled just having the chance to pick beans in the garden or wander through a plot of ground with watermelons lying in the sun. The sight of all those watermelons of varying sizes was worth having to dodge yellow jackets hovering above the ripening fruit.

Across town lived Uncle Earl and Aunt Louise and their four children. If ever I had a soul sister it was their daughter, Lisa. She seemed as miserable at her house as I was at mine. She visited us one summer and stayed as long as she could convince her parents to let her.

An aura of sadness surrounded Lisa. She constantly busied herself cleaning or cooking or babysitting. Always eager to please, Lisa treated me with kindness and seemed to enjoy visiting with us. I wondered why. Mamma and Daddy yelled at each other continuously, and how could she enjoy scrubbing and working when she's on vacation?

"It's different when it's someone else's house," she explained. I never found that to be so, except that I had never seen another house as dirty as ours. I looked forward to her visit the next summer. She cheerfully helped me with my chores and fixed my hair in different ways. Having Lisa around seemed like having an older sister.

During her second visit, Lisa became extremely upset and called her parents to come for her. She told me she would not be coming back. I thought she was mad at me and I couldn't stand the idea of spending every summer without her company. Lisa had tears in her eyes when she assured me I had done nothing wrong, but she would not give me a reason for her decision. Mamma said she was older now and had friends of her own age and better things to do with her time during the summer months. I knew a bigger reason chased her away, and I suspected my father had something to do with it, though I never had any proof. She was six years older than me, but she remained throughout my childhood my favorite person to visit when we went to her town.

Louisiana's climate paralleled Georgia's: steamy, hot, dry and dusty. Most of the roads in the near vicinity of my relatives remained unpaved dirt paths just big enough for two vehicles to pass. I loved to walk barefoot and feel the loose dirt's coolness when the evening sun had passed behind the horizon and taken with it the road's heat.

Most of the time the heat killed any desire to do much of anything. Such was the case during one summer's visit. Abbie, Mary Kate, and I were suffering from severe boredom when Abbie suddenly had an idea. "We could go see how Honey and Sugar are doing. Do you want to?" she asked of me and her sister, or perhaps she was asking either of us who might be willing.

"I don't care," I shrugged. "How far is it?" I didn't want to walk a long way in the heat.

"Not far," Abbie hollered back over her shoulder. She was already headed for the kitchen to ask her mother.

I supposed Honey and Sugar to be someone's dogs or horses and I wasn't particularly fond of either, so I had not bothered to ask who they belonged to until we were walking to see them.

"They don't belong to anyone," Abbie laughed. "They live with each other."

Noting my confusion, my older cousin explained, "Honey and Sugar are two old colored ladies."

I swallowed hard, remembering every horror story I had ever heard about colored folk. I was especially fearful of the one that warned, "If you touch a nigger you will turn black yourself."

"Is that their real names?" I asked, trying to camouflage my fear.

"No. Everyone just calls them that because they make the best tea cakes and they always have some made for the children who stop to see them," Abbie said. It sounded like a bribe to me. "Have you ever been inside their house before?" I asked suspiciously.

"Lots of times. We've known them for years," Mary Kate assured me.

I walked along in silence trying to figure a graceful way out of going into their house. Time ran out and I was still working on a solution when Sugar answered Mary Kate's knock.

"Lawd, have mercy!" she said, holding the door open for us and smiling from ear to ear. "Honey, it's Miz Abbie and Miz Mary Kate and a new 'lil friend," she said.

I had never been inside a Negro's house before, so I followed my cousins gingerly, half expecting the floor to open up and swallow me.

"And who dis ju done brought wid ju?" Honey asked, also

smiling. Abbie introduced me but I was struck dumb, unable to respond to her cordial greeting. I chose instead to bite my bottom lip and memorize every knot hole in the wood plank floor.

"De cat done gone and got ju cuzn's tongue. Dat's what done happened for sho!" Sugar said emphatically, arms crossed over her ample bosom.

"Well, maybe she feel more like talkin' after she git some of our tea cakes, sister," Honey said with a twinkle in her eye and slowly nodding her head. She said to Abbie and Mary Kate, "I know what ju two doin' here. You ain't done walk down here in dis here heat jus' to pass de time o'day wid two old ladies, now did ju?"

"Humph! Don't make no difference why dey come over, sister. Dey's here. And as long as dey here, dey may as well have some tea cakes and iced tea. I wuz jus' about to have some m'self." Sugar set the table for everyone in the room while Honey explained to me, "Ever' day after school some of de children what lives aroun' here stops in for a visit. Sho do brighten up our day, don't it sister?"

"Yes, Lawd. Where you two been keepin' yoselfs? You ain't been down in a long while. We thought you done forgot about us." Sugar pretended to have her feelings hurt.

"We been helping Mamma and Daddy put up the garden," Mary Kate answered. "But we would never forget about you and Honey."

"Not as long as ju got a sweet tooth in yo head!" Honey beamed.

"We would still come see you even if you didn't have anything sweet to eat," Mary Kate said reassuringly.

"Well, do tell! One dese days we jus' gone be fresh out and see do ju still come back!" Honey teased.

"Chile, ju better eat yo' cookies," Sugar said to me. "Ju don't eat somepin' and 'ole Honey gone get her feelings hurt."

"Side's dat," Honey piped in, "Abbie gone eat 'em all up, ju not careful."

"They go on like this all the time," Abbie said dramatically.

I had just begun to feel comfortable and enjoy the down-home atmosphere, when Abbie said we should go. As we stood near the door saying good-bye, the impossible happened. One of the sweet old ladies took one of my hands between her own and patted it. I felt the floor sway under my feet, and I was sure if I looked down I would see my hands growing darker if not already completely black. "Ju come back 'n see us what time ju find yoself back in dese parts," I heard Honey saying.

"I may have to!" I thought wildly. "I don't know any other place to go if I turn black!"

My cousins seemed so oblivious to what had just happened. On the way home I could stand it no longer, and I mustered the courage to say, "My brother told me once that you would turn black if a colored person touches you."

They howled with laughter. "That's the dumbest thing I ever heard!" said Abbie.

"It just isn't true," my older and more mature cousin said. I felt a rush of relief. After all, my skin still looked the same color it had always been. Then I remembered my mother saying when you get to be a teenager your body changes, and you become whatever you are going to be when you are an adult. Maybe they just didn't know about that. Maybe I would still turn black! I comforted myself with the thought that at least I had a few years to think about it and figure out what to do.

I told no one else about my fear, but I was extremely relieved to get back home to Marietta where things were familiar and everyone was white. I had bad dreams about waking up black, but in the relative comfort of familiar surroundings I told myself I could handle it somehow if it happened.

Janet was glad to see me. She had been very bored in my absence. She and I looked forward to Saturdays, for on that day her mother went to the dime store and bought material remnants for me to make into doll clothes for Janet's dolls. Little half yard pieces of crisp dotted swiss and perky calico, dainty pima cotton and warm flannel. How she and I looked forward to those weekly goody bags. Sometimes they contained bits of lace or teeny, tiny buttons. Janet told me what she wanted, and I tried to make it just that way.

It intrigued me that flat pieces of fabric could be turned into frilly dresses with puffed sleeves and lacy collars. We made everything: flowered nightgowns and practical play clothes, sheets for her doll's bed and pillow cases to match. It did not matter that we had only an imaginary pillow to go inside. We made it the size we thought it should be and spread it at the top of the bed anyway.

Sometimes I failed miserably in trying to make exactly what Janet had in mind, but she never complained. Once I messed up our project so badly, it couldn't be salvaged. When I finally worked up the courage to tell Mrs. Jones I had ruined the material she bought, she laughed and said, "I'll get some more next time I go to the store". No anger, no disappointment, no lecture.

A longing to be able to sew as well as Granny and Mamma grew inside me. I could do fine hand sewing. All Janet's doll clothes were made by needle and thread, but I wanted to use the real sewing machine, and I wanted to make real clothes. Mamma taught me by letting me make pajamas for my brothers. Since no one ever saw us in our pajamas, it didn't matter too much what they looked like. Within months, she trusted me to make clothes for myself and my brothers that would be seen by other people. I developed quite an attitude that I could do anything as well as anyone else could.

My mother's talent for sewing was something to be

admired. She had imagination and creativity and enough skill to transfer those attributes into dresses for me. She loved having a little girl to dress up, and I was a willing accomplice. My cooperation ended there, however.

It was one thing to wear the beautiful dresses she created. It was another thing entirely to sit still to have my hair fixed. Mamma wanted me to have beautiful, soft curls and I did once. Now my baby curls had given way to straight, thick, light brown hair. Only a few golden highlights remained to remind her of what used to be. She spent long periods of time rolling my hair, only to have the curl fall out an hour later. She bought soft pink foam rollers for me to sleep in so the curl would last through Sunday School and church. It never did. I liked it straight and long. Unfortunately, so did Daddy.

Nowhere was Mamma's creativity more on display than at our birthday parties. The house would be lavishly, though not expensively, decorated to carry out the theme of the party. For my ninth birthday, the guests were requested to come in costume to represent a comic strip character from the newspaper. I chose "Granny" from my favorite Sunday funnies. My mother appropriately dressed me in garb made by her diligent hands. She designed the homemade sheetcake with chocolate icing to look like a newspaper. The headlines, written in lettering of white icing read, "Karen Passes Ninth Year Mark".

Another year we dressed as characters from Mother Goose rhymes. My favorite by far was the year we came to the party dressed as what we wanted to be when we grew up. Mamma had baked into the cake little trinkets to represent the occupations of the men we were to marry. Before eating it, she instructed us to search carefully in our piece of cake for the dime representing a rich man, a toy ring meaning we would marry a jeweler, or the tiny facsimile of an animal for the girl destined to match up with a veterinarian. The airplane was for a Lockheed employee and so on. I loved my friends' outfits. They were for the moment, nurses, school teachers, ballerinas, and mommies carrying baby dolls. Of course, I wanted to be one of the mommies. I never aspired to be anything else. My brothers enjoyed pirate parties during which the guests searched for hidden treasures outside or sports parties where they dressed as baseball or football players, race car drivers, etc.

For all the time and effort invested in these parties, I was truly grateful. Yet every year I begged my mother not to make me have a party. For my sixth birthday, the girls from my kindergarten class had been invited. Sometime during the festivities my father threw a fit because one boy, the brother of the girl across the street, had come with his sister to the party.

"You didn't tell me there was going to be boys here!" he bellowed at my mother. "You call his mamma right now and get him out of here, and don't you ever bring any boys around Kayron again!" She didn't call anyone, and he stormed out of the house, staying gone until the party ended. I thought I would die from embarrassment, and I wished for the ground to open up and swallow me. His insensitive, drunken behavior shamed my mother, hurt my friends' feelings, and brought on the first of many migraine headaches for me.

Never again did I wish to bring a friend into my house. Every succeeding birthday party drove me to the bathroom with severe headaches accompanied by nausea and vomiting. I dreaded the big day from the moment the plans were made. I lived in mortal fear of Daddy looking up the girls' dresses or even worse, touching them the way he touched me sometimes. Mamma said I was silly to get so worked up over my birthday and she admonished me to "Don't be silly. You'll have a good time!" I never did, because my father made it a point to be at every party so he could be on the lookout for unwelcome boys.

My physical ailments did not limit themselves to birthday

parties. In fact, the headaches were so frequent and of such intensity, the school insisted I be taken to a doctor. My mother was furious. My father, a closed-mouthed man who gave few opinions and didn't much care how the money was spent anyway, stayed out of it. In the end, Mamma took me to Dr. Alden because she knew he wouldn't do any tests and it wouldn't cost her much money. Finding the cause or treatment of the problem did not seem to be important to her .

"Well, what's the problem, little lady?" The sweet, handsome face of the doctor inquired.

"She's been having headaches. I give her aspirin but the school says it's been going on too long and she's got to see a doctor. It's a sorry day when the public school can tell you how to raise your children."

He was asking *me*. He looked at me now. "Does anything make your headache worse? Does it hurt more when you do certain things?"

"No. It comes and goes," my mother answered for me. He was asking *me*. I wanted to tell him it hurts more when Daddy is home, and it hurts more when people yell at me. He walked behind me and patted me on the head and raised my thick hair in his hand.

"Look at this, Mamma," he said to her. "Your head would hurt too if it was this tiny and carrying around this much weight." He cupped my chin in his hand and said to me, "Honey, my professional opinion is you got too much hair. Get Mommy to cut about a foot off the length and I think your head will feel better. If it don't, come back and see me. We'll find out what's causing the problem if it isn't your hair."

Royal battles ensued over the issue of my crowning glory. Mamma insisted it be cut enough to do some good but long enough to keep Daddy happy. Daddy insisted if she cut one hair on my head he would never forgive her, and she would be sorry. Nobody asked me what I wanted... yet.

There was a big void in my visit to Granny's house that summer of 1958. I was surprised and upset to learn Robin no longer lived in town. Granny explained to me that Robin got married, had a baby, and now lived in another state with her husband who was in the Army. I felt cheated.

"She didn't tell me she was going to get married," I lamented.

"She didn't tell nobody. She jest up and did it. If you think you feel bad, how do you think her Ma feels?" Granny was upset over the unexpected turn of events too. I didn't know how Robin's mother felt, but I gathered by the sadness in her face that she must be taking it pretty hard. "I don't know what got into Robin," Granny said. "I don't know what it takes for young people to realize they need an education 'fore they start a family." Granny shook her head and left the room. I sat alone, trying to figure out for myself why my friend got married and moved away without even telling her mother.

I made up the time I might have spent with Robin by learning to cook. Granny decided if I wanted a cobbler every day I spent at her house, it was time I learned to make it myself. When I was not feeding my emotions with blackberry or peach cobbler, I was into Granny's favorite staple, sweet potatoes. There seemed to be a never-ending supply in her little patch of a garden, and we gleaned many late night snacks from the potato tub on the back porch.

We removed the skins with two dime store paring knives that had to be sharpened on the whet stone every time we used them. Then we sliced the potatoes into round circles a quarter inch thick before frying them in hot oil. Handling them covered our hands with a sticky orange stain that would not wash away.

"It'll wear off," Granny assured me.

After sprinkling the finished product with white sugar, we sat before the TV watching Granny's favorite shows and eating to our heart's content. The first time I learned to prepare those golden gems the way we liked them best was one of the highlights of my childhood. I suffered from a superiority complex for days, and Granny suffered from a steady diet of fried sweet potatoes, which I prepared with every meal. We sat side by side in the front porch swing eating a plate of them when Granny said, "I was thinking we might go get yore hair cut later today."

"Yes!" I squealed with excitement. I had been wanting it cut for a long time.

"How short do you want it cut, Katie?"

"I don't know," I answered. It never occurred to me that I had a choice.

"Well, you better decide before we get there. Alberta's about the sweetest person on earth and she'll fix yore hair jest like you want it. Do you want a permanent in it?" Now that was a new idea.

"Does it cost the same?"

"No, but you don't worry about that. I'm paying for it so that part ain't none of yore business. You jest worry about how you want it fixed." I knew Granny did not have much money and she did not waste money on extras. I pressed her for a price, but got nowhere. Finally, she said it cost about the same as one doctor visit, but if getting rid of my hair would get rid of my headaches it didn't matter how much it cost.

"Mamma will be mad if you pay for it, so I better not," I said.

"Yore Ma took you to the doctor and he said to get yore hair cut. I'm jest doin' what the doctor ordered."

"Daddy will be mad." I just thought she should be warned.

"You let me handle yore Pa," she said as she looked over her glasses and continued her steady rhythm swinging back and forth. "Yore too little to be tangling with him."

"He'll be really mad at you."

"I declare, Katie, sometimes I think you were put on this earth jest to argue!" Granny said, exasperated. "Forget about what everybody else says about yore hair and think about how you want it to look. I'm goin' to tell yore Ma and Pa it was my doin's, and they better not say a word to you about it."

Alberta proved to be everything Granny said she was and more. She gave me books to look at and helped me choose a cut I liked, and between customers she talked to me as if I were grown up. The curling rods dangled ominously by electrical wires daring me to have my head connected to them. "Does it hurt much to get a perm?" I asked.

"Oh, honey. It doesn't hurt at all, but now if you're tender-headed, I'll make sure I'm extra careful when I roll you," she said reassuringly. She showed me how the electric rollers clamped over the hair to bake in the perm solution. "If it gets to feeling too warm on your head, I'll turn the electric fan on where it will blow on your head and cool it off. Now the permanent solution is pretty strong and the fumes from it might make your eyes water, but I'll give you a cloth to hold over your eyes in case you need it." She was so reassuring in her rambling get-it-all-said-quickly style, I couldn't turn down the prospect of a whole new look.

She had one curler on the right side wound too tightly. It pinched but I didn't want to hurt her feelings by saying so. Mamma did that a lot, but it usually worked its way loose so I didn't complain. It began to feel too warm for my comfort almost immediately, but Alberta had become swamped with customers and I didn't want to bother her. Granny had left to run an errand while we waited for the perm solution to "take". Actually it wasn't uncomfortable all over, just on the right side. It felt like a hot roller was touching my ear, but I could bear it. Suddenly, the pain began getting worse by the second. For the next twenty minutes or so I clenched my teeth together, ignoring the burning pain while tears fell like silent rain. Because pain was such an integral part of my existence, I believed it was something one had to tolerate when it occurred. I did not interpret pain as a signal that something was wrong.

When Alberta came to check my curls, she said, "Sweetheart, is something wrong?"

"No," I lied.

"Well, that solution must be just tearing your eyes up, honey. You didn't get any in your eye, did you? Well, let me get you a wet cloth for your eyes. You just have a few more minutes." She brought a fan so it could blow the fumes back from my face.

At long last, Granny came back and it was time to take the rollers from my hair. As Alberta unrolled me she told Granny how my eyes had watered so bad and how she worried about the solution irritating them. Suddenly she gave a long gasp as I sat gripping the edge of the chair. Granny instantly jumped to her feet. "What is it?" she asked as she made her way to Alberta's side. When Alberta removed the clamp, part of my ear came off with it and stuck to the clamp. In her haste in rolling my hair, she had caught the top edge of my ear between the roller and the clamp.

Alberta started crying and saying she would take me to the doctor, whereupon I started crying and begging them not to. Granny didn't know who to comfort first. In the end, we put some Vaseline on my burn to keep the air from hurting it, and Granny doctored it herself when we got home. Eventually, my ear healed as good as new.

I secretly grieved over the loss of my hair. Truthfully, I had liked it the way it was. I just didn't want my father to like it. I hated the short cut, but I would never have admitted that. My headaches did disappear except for an occasional migraine, and for the first time, I felt a sense of power over my father. He could not control every part of me. My grandmother had given

*85*

me the right to choose for myself how to wear my hair, and in so doing she symbolically taught me that I was the one in charge of my life.

Daddy became distant and viewed me with disgust. When he finally chose to speak to me again, he did so only through derogatory comments about my hair and my character. Because of my lack of loyalty as his daughter, he said, he was considering taking a job in New York for a year. Actually, he had a choice of taking a contract for a job there or being laid off again.

To my great joy, he went to work somewhere in New York for almost a year. I began to feel different in his absence. I became more aware of my surroundings and myself. My relationship with my mother improved, and though she would never admit it, she shared our happiness in having him gone. To her eternal credit, she allowed me to pursue my own interests which, as always, were school work and sewing.

January brought with it my tenth birthday, the first one I could remember without feeling ill. As in all the previous years, I did not want a birthday party. For once, Mamma allowed me to skip the festivities she preferred to provide. Instead, she baked a cake, and Janet came to eat a piece with my brothers and me. Mamma blamed my lack of enthusiasm for a party on the fact that Daddy would not be there to celebrate with us. She seemed to forget that I had always asked to not have a party. I shook my head and decided that she was going to believe what she wanted to believe. I did not try to tell her anymore how I felt about anything.

I wanted to make her an Easter dress that year as a surprise. Another dress of hers served as a model for cutting the pattern. Since I couldn't use her to make sure the bodice length would be just right, I opted to make a skirt and blouse instead. She entrusted a few dollars to my care when I told her I wanted to buy her a surprise for Easter. That was a big step for her, since dollars were scarce and she had no idea what I wanted the money for.

The fabric store was my utopia, and I must have spent a good two hours there picking out the pale lavender cotton and lacy trim. There were so many decisions! What I originally had in mind suddenly seemed too youthful for her. I didn't want her to be embarrassed to wear it after I made it, and I wanted her to really like it. Would she want this color? She didn't have anything that remotely resembled it, yet I felt she would like it. Would this lace be too much? Not if I only put it on the collar and the hem of the overblouse, I decided.

It never crossed my mind to doubt my ability to create just what my imagination conceived. My biggest worry was sewing on it while Mamma was at work and keeping it hidden from her the rest of the time. I gave it to her the night before Easter so she could make last minute changes if it didn't fit just right. She was genuinely thrilled and surprised, and exhibited obvious pride in me and her new dress. I told her she didn't have to wear it on Easter Sunday if she would rather wear the other dress she had planned to wear. Mamma's sincere response assured me she wouldn't think of wearing anything but the one I made. She could not wait to show it off. She told everyone her daughter made it for her without even a pattern.

A strange sense of pride engulfed me, and for the first time I felt I had done something worthwhile. After years of being told to stifle my pride, my mother seemed to be saying it was okay to take satisfaction in my work, if not myself. She even sprang for a long distance call to tell Granny about it. I thought the outfit seemed a little big on her, although she assured me it was just perfect. Her genuine pleasure from my gift to her made up for hurtful things she had said to me in the past. I forgave and forgot them in the pure love of a child for her mother.

I hoped my father's stay in New York would somehow

mark an end to our past family life and the beginning of a different relationship. I missed what we had never had with a passion.

Mamma said Micah's behavior would improve when Daddy came home. He had begun "running with the wrong crowd" as she said. The police brought Micah home on several occasions, because they picked him up for vagrancy and vandalizing graveyards. Each time, Mamma rushed to his defense, claiming the police were harassing her son. She said you couldn't expect a twelve-year-old boy to be any different when his father had to be gone for months at a time just to put food on the table. She said a boy that age needs his father. Her message was clear. Males are not responsible for their behavior. There is always an understandable reason for their wrongdoing. Females, on the other hand, have no excuse for deviating from the straight and narrow path.

Randy apparently did not suffer the same ill effects from Daddy being gone. He played happily with his friends and kept himself constructively entertained. He was the clown of the family and everything was an adventure and everything was funny to him. He dealt with life by laughing in its face and daring it to hurt him.

Jeff seemed to benefit the most. Before Daddy left home, Jeff had started stuttering to the point we could hardly understand him. That had now almost completely disappeared and he became talkative and outgoing. Now three, he was the darling of the neighborhood with his beautiful blond hair and blue eyes.

Meanwhile, I had been doing a lot of Bible study and even more thinking. Mamma said, "It don't hurt to think as long as you keep your opinions to yourself." I decided the games Daddy played were wrong. I had developed a guilty conscience over that, and I promised God I would never let it happen again, no matter what.

# Chapter Seven
## * * *

Janet invited me to sleep at her house the night before she went to the hospital for eye surgery. Glaucoma had claimed her sight in one eye some time ago, and antibiotics had failed in their attempt to heal the ulcerated organ, now swollen to twice its size.

I didn't want Janet to be afraid, and I didn't want her mother to worry. It must be awful to know you are going to have your eye cut out of your body. Mrs. Jones stood at the head of Janet's bed putting drops in her daughter's eyes. I wished I could tell them I would be praying for Janet to be okay during the surgery, but my lack of social skills prevented any expression of sympathy. My family was so programmed to not talk about unpleasant things it was impossible for me to break the code of silence, especially to share a sentimental side of myself.

At twelve, Janet's mind had already reached its reasoning capacity. The mental retardation was evident, as were the physical deformities. Her feet curved inward and her reed-like legs struggled to hold up her weight. She could still walk unassisted, though haltingly. One could only guess if the bone structure in her legs was the culprit, or if her fading vision caused the uncertainty of her steps. Already blind in her bad eye, she saw only light and shadows with her good one.

"You're awfully quiet tonight, Miss Karen. Do you need

anything?" Mrs. Jones asked. I shook my head no. I wanted to say something comforting, or more likely I wanted someone to say something comforting to me. I remembered the night before I went to the hospital when I was three. I didn't want Janet to be scared. Emphysema made the operation more risky. I feared they wouldn't put her to sleep good enough, and she would feel them cut her eye. I should have known, though I didn't, that her parents had taken care of those details with the doctor beforehand. They had told her everything she needed to know to prepare for the operation. Janet's attitude was great. I was terrified for her.

As she tucked us into the twin beds, Mrs. Jones looked at me and said, "Say a prayer for Miss Janet tomorrow."

"I will," I said, smiling suddenly.

It was beyond my comprehension why they called the operation a success. Not only could Janet still not see, but now she had a sunken-in place where her eye used to be. She had outlived the doctor's prediction that she would be dead years ago. They spoke now of the possibility of her surviving to adulthood. We would have to wait and see.

* * * * *

Ever since Daddy came home from working up North, he eyed me with suspicion, frequently asking who I had been with while he was gone. I tried to tell him about school activities and my new friend, Jane, who moved in down the street a few months back. I thought he might want to know about new things Janet and I had learned to do.

"That ain't what I'm talking about and you know it," he said. "Has there been any boys in this house?"

"Just Micah's friends," I answered, missing his point entirely. With childish persistence, I still pursued the elusive dream of father-daughter communication. How I longed to have a conversation with him without the anger he wore like an identifying cloak! I wanted to tell him about the really neat go-cart Micah and his friends had built, but Daddy couldn't get past the thought of Micah's friends coming home with him the whole time Daddy had been away.

"Who were they? Did they say anything to you? Did anybody hurt you?" he asked savagely. I rationalized his jealousy by hoping his anger was not directed at me, but rather at anyone who may want to make me unhappy. Daddy really changed while he was away. I had convinced myself of that. I knew it must be true because Daddy had been home almost a week now and had not tried to touch me except for a hug when he first came home, and then it was the same kind of hug he gave everyone else in the room. How I longed to be held protectively in his arms and have him assure me he would take care of me.

"Did any of those boys say anything to you?" he repeated more calmly now.

"Bobby said no girls are allowed to watch. He said I had to go inside while they built the go-cart. I told him when my Daddy got home he would be sorry." I tried valiantly to play on Daddy's sympathy. He sat down on the couch with his hands dangling limp between his knees. I slid onto the couch beside him and put my arm around his neck.

"Will you tell him he can't come up here anymore?" I wheedled. Bobby really was one of my favorites of Micah's friends, but I wanted to milk this opportunity for paternal sympathy for all it was worth.

"Never mind him," Daddy said with a small smile. He pulled the afghan from the back of the couch and spread it over his lap. "Go get a blanket for you and you can sit here with me till your Mamma gets back with the boys. Then you'll need to help her get supper ready."

Excitement built as I surveyed this new daddy. From all indications the games were a thing of the past, and now I would have a daddy I liked and could trust. It was going to be great sitting beside him, watching television like everyone else I knew did with their daddies. With blanket in hand, I climbed onto the couch beside him and he playfully mussed the top of my hair.

I enjoyed the closeness. I thought I would enjoy staying there all day. After a few minutes, he patted his lap. "Climb on up here on my lap. It's O.K.," he said reassuringly. When I hesitated, he tried to coax me with his words. A familiar feeling of suspicion returned. When I resisted, he deftly wrestled my panties from my body and pulled me onto his lap facing him. I realized too late that he had undone his pants and covered himself with the afghan when he sent me for another blanket.

"NO!" I said. "I can't do that anymore!"

"What do you mean you can't do it anymore? It's just like before. Just sit still," he said insistently.

My legs hurt from being spread too far apart. He wrapped both arms around my back and shoulders and jammed me downward onto himself. I felt the same old burning, tearing pain and my body shuddered and convulsed as the familiar choking sound formed in my throat while I fought to suppress a scream. To my own surprise, I didn't care anymore if someone found out. My body had been free of pain for a whole year, and it rebelled against the sudden onslaught. The scream, hidden now for ten years, rose and built to its peak, both frightening and angering my father in its unexpectedness.

"I told you never to make a noise!" I heard as I felt his hands gripping my throat, cutting off my air supply. My attention swung from the diminishing pain in my mid-section to the growing pain in my throat. The desperate need to breathe brought an urgent desire to retaliate. No longer did I simply want my own protection. Suddenly I wanted to strike back, to hurt him, not because of the physical pain he caused me, but because his betrayal had shattered with absolute certainty my hope of ever being a little girl with a daddy who really cared about me.

Daddy was stronger than I remembered. He had not been drinking, and without the alcohol in his system, I would never be able to fight him. I remembered I should call for help, which was impossible under the circumstances. Still, I reached for the phone on the end table just to my right. Instinctively, I hit him in the face with the receiver as hard as I could. On the first blow, blood gushed from above his eye. Daddy let go of me and touched his head with his finger.

"Now look what you've done!" he spat the words, throwing me like a crumpled piece of paper onto the floor. He dashed to the bathroom to inspect the damages and I sat, crying now, gripping my panties he had removed from me earlier.

I knew I had to leave quickly, but where would I go? If I stayed, Daddy might kill me. If I left, I would have to explain to Mamma. If I told her the truth, she would say I exaggerated the incident, and she would hate me for it. I was afraid to leave, but I was even more afraid to stay.

I housed myself that night in an empty building that had once been rented by Jane's aunt when she sold antiques from there. The only thing that scared me more than Daddy was snakes. I tried to not think about them as I made my way behind the row of houses across the street and through the field of overgrown weeds to the darkened, eerie building standing forlorn in the twilight. I worried about what I would do if it were locked up tight, but the doors were unlocked and slightly ajar. I was immensely relieved to find it so easily accessible.

There were, I learned, many places to go, but nowhere to be absolutely safe or warm or loved. Had I ever felt safe, even in the womb? I wondered. Had that liquid abode of prenatal days been a haven for me or just a prelude of things to come?

I tell people I left home at the age of ten. That isn't exactly true. It would be more accurate to say I left hope at the

93

age of ten. For the next few years, I volleyed between sleeping at home to make Mamma happy and sleeping various other places when I could stand it no longer. I probably spent an equal amount of time at home as I did elsewhere, but it was a full-time job planning where I could sleep if it were not safe enough at home that night.

A nearby field afforded me a second home during fair weather. The tall grasses camouflaged my dwelling place, a beaten down area of weeds near a small grove of trees. A few scraggly blackberry bushes offered juicy fruit a few weeks each summer, and several plum trees provided more than enough fruit for me and the variety of birds who came to feast.

Early morning dew covered me as completely as it did everything else in the field around me. In the pre-dawn chill of my newfound home, I sat with my arms wrapped around my knees and listened to the chatter of birds bringing the world to life. Ironically, it was in this besotten condition that I spent my first "dry" night. For almost eleven years I wet my bed every night. Only when I left home and slept alone under the stars did I manage to control my bladder while I slept.

One evening as I made my way to my home away from home in the growing darkness, a car loaded with young men watched me go into the field. They stopped their vehicle and followed as I picked a path through the tall weeds. The first faint tremors of fear grew to full fledged terror as I listened to their taunting comments. From their words and their mannerisms I knew they did not intend to leave me alive. It was too late to turn back, for I would surely run directly into the six men. Ahead lay only woods.

I ran a short distance, then fell flat with my ear pressed hard against the ground as they closed in around me. My throat constricted with fear as weeds swished back and forth in response to the invading footsteps. My white-knuckled fingers desperately gripped clumps of grass as my peripheral vision

**94**

caught a glimpse of the group's leader. My enemies were now within a few feet of me. If I could see them, I knew they could see me.

"Here she is. I got her. She's mine first."

"And I'm next," a second man smirked. I heard the unmistakable sound of someone unbuckling his belt. The leather sang across the fabric of his pants as he jerked it through the belt loops.

Then, miraculously, the men seemed to lose sight of me simultaneously. Suddenly, one of the men shouted vulgarities as he inquired of the others, "Where'd she go?"

"She's got to be here somewhere," said another.

"This is crazy. I just had my eye on her."

"Keep looking. She ain't gettin' away that easy."

I lay still and quiet, convinced the sound of my pounding heart would give me away.

Then, for no apparent reason, one of the men became terrified as he pointed just above where I lay and stumbled backwards. More profanity followed. Then the ringleader called out, "Let's get out of here! Now!" It seemed to me the ground shook as they thundered across the field. Car doors slammed and tires squalled as the pursuers became the pursued by some force invisible to me.

Though I never saw an angel nor heard the voice of one, I was comforted by a presence so real I felt that someone was holding me in his or her arms. But the blessed relief lasted only briefly. Like one waking from anesthesia, reality slowly traded places. I lay trembling, still afraid to move. But the earthy smells kissing my nostrils, the hardness of the ground, and the gentle wind blowing across my face all brought me back to full awareness of my surroundings and moved me to action.

My fingers were stiff and painful from gripping the ground, and I was so weak from relief, I could only lay there and cry for a few moments before survival instincts took over.

I rose from my hiding place, slowly, as one waking from a dream. I valiantly tried to crouch on hands and knees that suddenly seemed made of gelatin and scanned the horizon just above the weeds for any sign of danger.

Had I imagined the whole thing? I'm going crazy, I thought. The strange marriage of fear and relief sent me into a dizzying spin. Had I hit my head? No, I'm just crazy, just like Micah says. More concerned about losing my mind than losing my life, I remained low to the ground and rubbed my temples to stabilize my vision. Objects came into focus and the serpentine outline of a man's belt lying in the weeds met my eyes. I whimpered and skirted on all fours around the belt like an animal backing away from a whip. I stood and fled into the street without thinking to look.

My second home was no longer any safer than my first home. I befriended two foster kids in our neighborhood who lived in separate homes. "My mother is at work, and my daddy is drunk, so I don't want to go home" usually guaranteed a free meal and a night's lodging with no questions asked.

During cold or rainy weather, I sneaked into a separate section of our basement away from where Daddy came to drink his vodka. The area was hardly more than a crawl space, but it did have a concrete floor and served a two-fold purpose. It provided dry shelter, and I could hear when Daddy left the house. I took advantage of those times when I knew Daddy was gone to return to the house to bathe and get clean clothes.

My little brothers either greeted me with tears of gladness or with stony silence, angry that I had not stayed to protect them. Jeff always begged me to stay at home. Guilt consumed me when I didn't. It was hard to ignore his pleading eyes. The sexual assaults on me did occur again after that point, but they trickled to very rare happenings. I did not know then that Daddy replaced me with my youngest brother and subjected Jeff to his frequent attacks when I was not available.

# Chapter Eight
### * * *

During this time period, while I roamed my childhood stomping ground looking for a safe place to be, the Reverend Martin Luther King Jr. marched across Georgia and Alabama proclaiming his people would overcome the injustice and oppression they had endured since the founding of our country. Like them, I was also struggling to be heard above the blind ignorance around me.

"I'd like to kill that nigger and shut his mouth up for good!" My father's voice echoed the sentiment of many white folks across the South. The black population spoke as one voice, too big to ignore any longer. Fear and prejudice, born generations before, had grown and festered until my generation of children were taught to avoid black people like the plague.

Micah's warning that "if you touch a nigger it will rub off on you. Then you will be as black as they are" had held me prisoner of suspense for a while. Though I no longer believed him, (after all, he was the only one I had ever heard say it) that thought-provoking comment started me on an imaginary journey into the world of black people. What would it be like to be black? News reports said their schools were atrocious and white people would not tolerate the condition of the schools for their own children. Daddy said "niggers" were too stupid to learn anyway, so they didn't need better schools. Mamma agreed and said they never took care of anything anyway.

Mamma said, "Martin Luther King Jr. just wants to stir up trouble, and besides, most niggers are happy just the way they are."

I looked into the faces that seemed to look back at me from our old black and white TV set. King's followers didn't look like troublemakers to me. They looked like people. I saw pain and suffering in the faces of black mothers as they held small children by the hand and marched silently along. Teenagers desperately wanting to go to college registered disappointment at being turned away. Yet I heard of white youth who were being made to go to college by their parents and were only there because they had to be. I was too young to understand the issues, but I was old enough to think that maybe black people weren't all bad, and we weren't altogether right. I could relate to their misery, though for different reasons. I, too, was at the mercy of some one higher up to give me my rights. I, too, knew despair, yet an undercurrent of hope.

The black-white, segregation-integration problem puzzled me. Some people said blacks were just as smart as whites. Others said they couldn't be taught. The adults in my world taught that God's will prohibited mixing races. Martin Luther King Jr. was a preacher, and a Baptist preacher at that. He had a goodness in his manner that the self-righteous Christians who were condemning him lacked. He didn't sound stupid to me. He sounded very smart. And educated. And wasn't that what Granny said was more important than almost anything else? I was going to ask her what she thought of this situation next time I saw her.

I developed a curiosity about people. All people. Even those I feared. Minority groups interested me most of all. Why were blacks lazy and shiftless? Or were they really? What made Japanese and Koreans shrewd business people, and why were Jews so tight with their money? Why did lily-white Christians stereotype everyone who wasn't exactly like themselves? Maybe Mexicans were dirty, but how did we know that? We didn't know any Mexicans. And why should we pity American Indians and accept them at all costs, according to my mother? Most confusing of all, why did Southern Baptists give so much money to foreign missions to help the natives in Africa, but snub the black people across town?

I was a rebel without a cause and sometimes I was given to wondering aloud about black people. On those occasions Micah called me a "nigger lover" which infuriated, and yet intimidated me. I learned somewhat to channel my curiosity into safe areas of exploration.

I found it more profitable to hold all questions until I visited Granny. Though she told me repeatedly that curiosity killed the cat, she never really seemed to mind answering questions or showing me how to do something. Even there, sometimes my curiosity got me into sticky situations. Like the time I wasn't sure what "RESET" meant exactly, so I pushed the button it was written on to find out. I had just finished pouring myself some ice water from the old glass jug in the refrigerator when I noticed the button above the freezer compartment.

"Aunt Hattie, what is this button for on the freezer?" I asked my grandmother's sister.

"It starts it defrosting. Don't touch it!" she called from the other room.

"I already did," I answered with a sick feeling in my stomach. The last thing I wanted to do was make her upset with me. Having to wait for a freezer to melt the thick coat of ice could take hours of constant dripping even if we set a pan of hot water inside it. I had helped with that process many times but never at 11:00 at night. The worst feeling in the world was knowing I had done something wrong. Why hadn't I waited for an answer instead of trying to figure it out myself?

I fell all over myself apologizing and assuring the two elderly ladies that I could take care of it. I begged them to go on to bed. I felt worse with every passing moment.

"Well, I guess we won't be going to bed after all," Aunt Hattie's observation began an exchange of frustration-fraught comments between the two of them which were all directed at me.

"Katie, I swear if you don't have to find out everything the hard way," Granny said as she filled the kettle with water and lit the stove. "But there ain't no sense cryin' over spilt milk."

"Go turn Johnny on," referring to Johnny Carson, host of The Tonight Show. " If we gone be up all night, we might as well have company."

This came from my aunt who, like my grandmother, wasn't really fussing at me, just thinking out loud how to make the best of a bad situation. So the three of us took turns emptying the pans we put under the freezer area and mopping up the mess. Later, as we climbed into bed, I threw out one last weak apology into the still darkness.

"Well, it had to be done sometime soon, anyway," Granny said, her voice weary with age and exertion.

"And now you know what that little button is for!" added Aunt Hattie.

Aunt Hattie was actually Granny's half-sister and had recently moved in with her. They thought they would be good company for each other. They were mistaken.

Aunt Hattie was younger than Granny but that did not stop her from telling Granny what she should do and how she should do it. (And Granny thought I was born to argue). Their many arguments, though comical, sometimes resulted in hurt feelings on both sides. Still, I loved Aunt Hattie's dry humor and her desserts. No one tried to compete with her coconut cake, and it always amazed me that she could eat so many sweets and still weigh only eighty pounds soaking wet. Like her older sister, she wore her gray hair pulled back into a bun. Her severe hunchback gave her a somewhat witch-like appearance, although it would have been hard for anyone not to like her.

Granny and Aunt Hattie had major quarrels over washcloths. Aunt Hattie was convinced Granny was trying to steal hers. Always the peacemaker, Granny said, "Well, I'll tell you what, sister!" her irritation evident, "you just get out the embroidery basket and mark an 'H' on everything you own and I'll embroider what belongs to me with a 'G'." Aunt Hattie never accused Granny of stealing them again.

We were especially tired the night after the defrosting episode. Mamma and Daddy had driven down to pick me up, and we were to leave the next day to go home. Mamma was hard of hearing and she wore a hearing aid during the day to correct the problem. Her hearing impairment allowed her to sleep through Daddy's nightly drunken blunderings, but the rest of us had a hard time getting to sleep.

Granny, Aunt Hattie, and I lay in the same bedroom talking to each other and taking turns yawning. When finally the back door slammed, Granny exclaimed, "Well, thank goodness. He'll get another drink and then he'll pass out for the night."

"Uh huh, what's left of it!" Aunt Hattie said.

"Granny, do all men drink?" I asked.

"I reckon they's a few that don't. But they's few and far between," she said.

"What about preachers?" I persisted.

"I don't imagine Baptist preachers do. If they do they don't let it be known," she answered.

Aunt Hattie interrupted, "If you two will quit yappin', I'm gone try to git to sleep while it's quiet."

We all three almost succeeded when Daddy stumbled back in, bumping every wall along the way and talking to some invisible companion. Finally his bedsprings creaked and his mumblings ceased. Then his shoe fell onto the hard wood floor.

"There's one," Aunt Hattie remarked.

"And there's the other one," Granny said some time later when the other shoe finally dropped. "Now let's git some sleep." Teetering on the edge of that now enticing state of semi-consciousness, I heard a noise like the last two.

"Well damn!" My aunt's voice exploded in the velvety darkness. "How many feet has he got?" Her voice revealed her frustration. I lay momentarily frozen by the tension and her unexpected and uncharacteristic cursing. Suddenly, I convulsed in laughter, and after several useless admonitions for me to be quiet, they both joined me in sporadic, uncontrollable mirth.

# Chapter Nine
## * * *

Shame weighed so heavily on my eyelids that I was unable to lift them to meet another human's gaze. Consequently, when someone talked to me, I busied myself doing something, anything to give me an excuse to keep my eyes from meeting theirs. Interpreted as rudeness or disinterest, it was far from either. I was very interested in people, but I was unable to talk to anyone face to face.

Shame paves a devastating road into adolescence. Stripped of self confidence, lacking in social graces, and carrying a load of guilt heavier than myself, I stumbled along the prescribed course set for me by society's expectations. I went to school with my peers. I sat in church with them, and I played with girls I had known all my life, but I was never part of them. My body was there, but my spirit and my mind were in a fog, unsure of my acceptance by the group.

I felt myself splitting into two people. One of me was unable to cope any longer with stressful situations, and I would escape them at all costs. If escape were not possible, I would eventually tremble, then cry uncontrollably until, finally, I hyperventilated and collapsed into a semi-conscious state. Then the *other me* took charge, and a stoic calm replaced the erratic behavior along with acute embarrassment over it. At this point in my life, giving control to the other personality differed from the earlier years. Previously, I alternated between simply pretending the other me was being abused instead of myself, or I had no awareness whatsoever when the other personality was present. Now both entities seemed to be present at the same time and were aware of each other.

Panama City became my escape hatch. Granny's house in Eufaula was safe, but not very exciting for a teenager. So many members of Granny's extended family lived in Panama City that a place to sleep and a warm welcome awaited us at any time. I could sit forever by the ocean. Even though it terrified me, its very constancy was reassuring. The waves rolled in. The waves rolled out. Night and day, year after year. The never-ending sound of the surf and the smell of salt water never failed to revive me physically and rejuvenate my spirit.

Ironically, high school proved both threatening and stabilizing. I had many girl friends, good friends of good character. Though I had no desire for a boyfriend, my ego desperately needed a boost from someone of the opposite sex.

Early in my freshman year, a new family moved in across the street. My father, intent on finding a drinking buddy, befriended the man of the house and promised him I would find his son, who was my age, a ride to school. That was a prized service in our neighborhood since we lived five miles from school, and the school bus picked up an hour before the school opened.

I protested, but eventually gave in to my father's demands that I walk over and meet the man's son. Mr. McClendon answered my knock and called to his son, "Teddie, someone to see you." He then dismissed himself, leaving the two of us alone on the front porch. Staring back at me with equal uneasiness was almost six feet of pencil thin insecurity. I knew it instantly.

"My father sent me to see if I could help you find a ride to school," I began. "He doesn't realize I don't have a ride myself, but I thought I would come and meet you."

Such began a hide-and-seek relationship. Ted left notes in my mailbox; I dodged him in the halls at school. He called me for dates; I was always busy. He moved away several times; I told him I was sorry to see him go. It was the polite thing to say. I chose to forget about him when he was not around and that was most of the time. His mother, a hyper-energetic woman who couldn't stay in one town for long, constantly moved the family from Georgia to California to Indiana. Her grown daughters by a previous marriage lived in the two other states. Her restlessness caused Ted to change schools every few months.

He turned out to be a great pen pal, and getting mail from far away places excited me. Besides, I craved attention, and Ted thought everything about me was wonderful. He even told me I was pretty, music to a young girl's ears.

Dot and Kermit Alberts were also new residents on our street. They acquired my name from their next door neighbor as a potential babysitter. They both worked nights and needed me to spend the night at their house and care for their three tiny daughters. At two months, one year, and almost two years, they all still wore diapers, but I more than willingly rose to the challenge. I found their soiled, wet cloth diapers infinitely preferable to Daddy's vodka-vomit, urine-semen stained underwear.

It proved to be an arrangement made in heaven. Kermit arrived home in the mornings just in time for me to leave for school. Dot helped secure a waitress job for me at the restaurant where she worked. I went directly there after school and worked until 10:00 p.m. at which time I came home to switch places with Dot so she could leave for work. The girls were all asleep at that time and I would spend the next few hours doing homework. Usually the school assignments would be finished before the youngest baby woke for her late night feeding.

An extremely light sleeper, I eventually learned to sleep through their benign baby whimpers, but rise immediately when they really needed me. Dot worried that I wouldn't get enough sleep, knowing at least the youngest one would wake every three or four hours for a bottle. I didn't tell her that three or four hours of uninterrupted sleep was a long time for me. Even when no danger lurked, my fear awakened me every hour or two until now. I felt I should be paying them room and board instead of them paying me for childcare.

Kim, Kathy, and Kristy soon won my heart, and I took them most everywhere I went on the weekends. Mamma was not happy that I rarely came home anymore. She said a fourteen-year-old girl ought to be home where she belonged. Daddy agreed, with an evil glint in his eye.

Early the next summer, Mamma chose to go to Panama City without Daddy. His health was failing now, the alcohol finally destroying his liver and his brain. I went to Florida with Mamma, and it was the best trip we ever had. She surprised me when she took me aside and asked if I would be interested in going out with a distant cousin that night. She said his mother had called to see if she would allow me to go.

"Which one is he?" I asked.

"Karen, you know who Brad is! Don't be silly. You see him every year," she chided.

True. I saw a lot of relatives every year, but I never paid any attention to any of them except Aunt Thelma and Uncle Rupert. As Thelma mixed bread dough at the kitchen counter, she answered for my mother, "Brad is the middle boy in the family, Carol." Aunt Thelma and Uncle Rupert always called me Carol. I never knew why and never minded that they did. "He's the only one of the three with blond hair. His brothers both have brown hair," she continued.

Brad. Yes, I remembered him now, but only as a young boy on my grandmother's back porch, not from having seen him just the day before.

"Where does he want to go?" I inquired.

"She mentioned a movie, but I don't know for sure," my mother replied.

"You mean like a date?" I stared transfixed with eyebrows raised and my mouth half open. I had never been on a date before, and I wasn't sure I wanted to now.

"Well, something like that, I guess, but since he's a third cousin I don't know if you would call it a date or not," she said.

"Why didn't he call and ask me himself?" I was finding fault already.

"He will. Joyce didn't ask me to ask you. She just asked if I would let you, but I wanted to know if you are interested before I call her back."

This felt strange. She had never given me a choice in anything before. Somehow I felt she wasn't really giving me one now, but it sure sounded like it. Maybe she was only asking me for appearances' sake. Her tone indicated she thought I should go.

"How long would we be gone?" I wanted to know.

"I don't know. Does it matter?" She was getting weary of my questions.

Thelma said as long as I was with Brad there was no need to worry about how late we stayed out. I found the idea of going out with Brad terrifying, but so exciting. I couldn't wait to tell Jane. I decided that even if I had a bad time, I would tell her it was great.

The young boy from Granny's back porch had grown up and had done it very nicely. His hair was still blond and his eyes were still blue, but he had grown to six feet and developed a very pleasant voice. Our date developed into an evening of polite verbal exchanges and for me, extreme nervousness. We both breathed a sigh of relief when the drive-in-movie started and we could divert our attention from having to make conversation. Amid scenes of "North To Alaska", we began to unwind somewhat. Stilted though the evening was, we had unknowingly laid the cornerstone for a mutual admiration. I felt sure the date had been his mother's idea, and I was grateful to her.

When the vacation ended, I worked full time during the day and took any other odd job offered to me. I worked hard at saving money. I wanted to be able to buy a used car when I turned sixteen. The transportation problem to and from school became more and more difficult. I rode the school bus only when I could find no other way. Walking between two rows of other teenagers on the bus to find a seat always left me shaken. My insecurity whispered, "Everyone is looking at you. They are staring at your clothes, your body, your acne!"

I stayed busy so I wouldn't have to think. I gave 100% effort to everything, compulsively making list after list, crossing off each goal I reached and planning new ones. I took every extra babysitting job I was offered, filling every hour and sometimes overlapping jobs and combining children if the parents approved.

I longed to wear makeup and fix my hair in an attractive style, an impossibility in my current emotional state. I still could not look in a mirror for more than a passing glance, certainly not long enough to apply makeup or style my hair. Mamma always said I should wash it, brush it, and let it go. Anything else constituted sin and vanity.

"Makeup is only for whores," Mamma said. I felt like everyone thought of me that way, anyway. I certainly didn't want to give them any food for thought.

Sometime in my sophomore year, I yielded to Ted McClendon's constant requests to go to a movie with him. A monumental mistake. He fell in love with me, and he thought I liked him more that I actually did. He was a nice guy and a good telephone buddy, but I didn't feel any connection to him.

I didn't feel any connection to anyone, but I longed to. I wanted more than anything to be normal and enjoy life. I found to my disappointment that I could not enjoy any part of life that other kids my age did. I joined clubs at school, bought a car, went to all the football games, and worked nonstop between other commitments. The forced smile on my face fooled my girlfriends. Strangely enough, I was the leader in my little group of friends and well-liked. Yet, happiness eluded me, and times of deep depression and a prevailing feeling of hopelessness overshadowed me.

When I felt I could no longer cope, I drove to Panama City for as many days as possible, sometimes only overnight. Brad graciously invited me to do things with him when he knew I was in town. By the end of summer, our friendship had grown, and I felt very comfortable with him.

*  *  *  *  *

Robin moved back to Eufaula with her husband and two children. They bought a house within walking distance of Granny's house. I had seen Robin change over the years until now she was almost always angry with someone, usually her husband. From my adolescent observations, he was mild-mannered, good-looking and hopelessly in love with Robin.

Because I loved Robin, I wanted to be with her. There were times, however, when her angry words frightened me and I had to cut our visits short. Her eight-year-old son and six-year-old daughter were both beautiful and very sweet children. Naturally, I enjoyed being with them. I knew Robin loved them very much, but sometimes she treated them mercilessly. It disturbed me to see her so torn, and I was too young to make any sense of her confusion. We connected on some level I could not discern. Her very confusion and like responses to certain situations seemed to say to me that she understood my pain and despair.

When boredom overtook us or the summer's heat became

too oppressive, Robin was ready at the drop of a hat to head for the creek for a cooling off period. I thought her husband must resent having to work so hard at his job every day while she was swimming in the creek. Because my mother had always been in charge of all the household duties and also worked a full time job, I had come to expect that all women should work and maintain the home. Robin believed that giving birth two times constituted enough work for one person for a lifetime.

"Don't ever get married, Karen. It's a total waste of energy and the only fun is in your mind. Do something with your life, for your own pleasure!"

Every time I visited Robin, I got a 'finish your education' speech from Granny. She knew how much I liked Robin, and I suppose she feared Robin's 'live for today' philosophy would rub off on me. So, several times a year, Granny told me to get an education so that I would never have to depend on anyone else for anything. "That's the one thing nobody can take away from you," she would say. "Whatever you learn is going to stay with you 'til the day you die. I don't want any of my grandyounguns to be ignorant on schooling like I am. I quit after the third reader and I've spent most of my life regretting it."

"But Granny, you're the smartest person I know," I protested.

"Well, there ain't no substitute for common horse sense, that's for sure," she said with a sigh. "You can't go too far without it. But you can be smart as a whip, and if you ain't trained for nothin', you might as well not even have the brains God give a billy goat for all the good it will do. The good Lord give you a healthy mind, Sugar. It's up to you to use it."

At least a dozen rebuttals came to mind, but I had the good sense to stifle them. One could argue with Granny if it were done respectfully, but you would end up looking stupid if you weren't careful. No matter how intelligent my ideas seemed in my head, they crumbled and fell away like desert sand when voiced before her power of reason.

Granny had everything I wanted in life that couldn't be assigned a dollar value. You couldn't buy friends or the devotion of your children and grandchildren. How could you educate yourself into having church members and neighbors stop by to visit whenever they passed your house just because they enjoy your company? I couldn't see that she had missed out on anything that really mattered by her lack of education. Certainly I wanted a bigger house. I would not be satisfied with a shack like the one she called home, but I knew in the depths of my soul that no house I would ever own would ever contain the happiness that lived within those pine-panelled walls.

Marietta became a trap for me. The city represented intolerable images that haunted me even in the relative safety of another family's house that I now called home, or in my car as I drove down the street. I couldn't wait to leave that town, and I made plans to attend a college as far away as I could qualify for. I took college prep courses in high school and longed for the day I could sprout my wings and fly away. I wanted to go to college in Florida, but geographically it was still too close to my immediate family, from whom I desperately needed to separate.

Anxiety attacks began to plague me, crippling me when I least expected it. I knew no one would understand, because I didn't. I assumed the fluttering heartbeat and chest pains were symptoms of heart problems. Since the thought of going to a doctor hopelessly terrified me, I would retreat to a little corner of the world and hope to die. Inevitably, the attack would pass and I would then be embarrassed and even more afraid of the next one. I spent more and more time in Panama City. Sometimes after severe anxiety attacks, I would drive six hours to Mexico Beach and sit alone at the healing edge of the beach recovering my sanity, until I felt normal enough to return to the ever present pressures of school, work, and family.

On happier occasions, when I knew ahead of time I was going, Joyce and Bill, Brad's parents, invited me to stay with them. Their house was a cocoon of safety where the innocence of childhood was content to slip away, conceding by bits and pieces to the tingling, tantalizing pull of adolescence. There, as in Eufaula, I could be me, whoever that was.

Brad saved me from emotional despair, and neither of us even knew it. He included me in his circle of friendship, and I would bask in his company. It made no difference where we went or what we did. As long as he remained nearby, my fears minimized, and my joy increased. Our relationship was so low key and non-committal I could not see the depth of positive impact he was having on my life. Relatives teased us about being kissing cousins, but their comments did not bother us. I enjoyed his company too much to really care. We knew our boundaries and never crossed the borderline. Besides, he was too much of a gentleman and I was too terrified of sex for there to be much basis for any rumors. Still, I was infatuated, as teenagers are prone to be. I had intense interest in anything he did or said, yet I did not desire a romantic involvement.

One day I mentioned to Brad that I needed to buy more suntan lotion. That night he wrote on the family message board, "Mom, pick up suntan lotion. - Karen." His parents had already gone to bed for the night, and that was their way of communicating with their hectic schedule of two working parents and three teenage boys. I vehemently protested leaving a message from me.

"She will know I wrote it. It's my handwriting," Brad said.

"It sounds so presumptuous," I replied.

"Go to bed," he ordered, turning off the light and motioning for me to precede him down the hallway. "You worry too much."

I laid in bed wondering what Joyce would think of me if she were to awaken to such a message - calling her "Mom", expecting her to do an errand for me, intruding on the family's private message board. I waited until everyone fell asleep, then made my way down the darkened hall to erase the message. What would it be like to be part of an easygoing family like this, I mused. There was no comparison between Brad's family and mine. I therefore drew the conclusion that there was no comparison between Brad and myself.

The next morning Brad glanced back at the blackboard as he walked past it and sat down opposite me at the kitchen breakfast bar. "Did you erase the message I put on the board last night?" he asked.

I searched for just the right words. "I thought it would be presumptuous of me... like I 'm trying to be part of this family."

"You are part of this family," he chuckled. His low, easy laughter took the edge off my intensity.

"Well, I just don't want your Mom to think I expect her to do something for me," I explained.

"She loves running errands for us," Brad teased. "It makes her feel useful."

"Mom, would you pick up some suntan lotion for Karen while you're out today?" he asked her moments later when she entered the room.

"Sure. You two going to the beach today?" she asked.

"Not if I can help it," Brad mumbled, grinning to show he was teasing.

"Actually, Karen, if you don't have more exciting plans I would like for you to go shopping with me."

So, while Brad ran some errands, his mother and I went shopping together. Over lunch, she prompted me to talk about my dreams and hopes for the future. This must be what it should be like with mothers and daughters, I thought. She gave me no reason to feel inferior, so why did I? She was kindness and generosity, so why did I not trust her motives?

"Are you having a good time this week?" she asked.

"Yeah. I'm not sure Brad is, but I am," I replied. "I think he may be letting me hang around with him just to be polite."

"I wouldn't worry about that!" his mother laughed. "I know Brad pretty well and if he weren't having a good time, he wouldn't take you out just to be polite." We both laughed as we considered the truth of her maternal knowledge.

"I finally figured out what it is I like about you," Brad said that evening as I slid into the passenger side of his car.

"Yeah, what's that?" I said, feeling an affectionate round of sarcasm on the horizon.

"I don't feel intelligent around too many people, but I feel smart when I'm with you. You give me a superiority complex."

"Face it, Brad. You like being with me because I make you look good," I responded with a confidence I didn't really feel. Sarcasm was in vogue in the 1960's, and it came as second nature to me. Brad usually had the last word in our little spats of verbal insults. His retorts did not offend me. On the contrary, I knew he considered me at least intelligent enough to understand sarcasm and respond in kind.

"Well, now that I'm sitting here looking so good, where do you want to go tonight?" he asked.

"Can we go to the beach?" He should have known I would say that. I always chose the solitude of the less popular areas of Mexico Beach over the more populated main strip of Panama City with its carnival rides and boat rentals. I thought he would have preferred the excitement of the night life and crowds somewhere else, but he never said so.

Brad claimed to be not much of a talker. Admittedly, he did not out talk me, but he did all right for himself. We rarely ever spoke of anything of real importance, but we kept up a stream of idle chatter and comfortable rapport. In his presence, I knew laughter and contentment. Both were new sensations for me. Being with him made me happy, especially when we were together at the beach at night. Only then was my secret miles away and I was almost Angela, the fabricated self-image from my childhood.

"Are you having a love affair with these sand dunes?" Brad asked as he politely took the lead, picking our way through the sea oats. "This is the third time we've been here this week."

"I like the beach," I shrugged.

"Why do you say you like the beach? You never even get your feet wet," he accused.

"I didn't say I like the ocean. I said I like the beach, as in shore and sand," I replied.

"Chalk one up for Karen in word games," he said.

I wasn't sure what he meant by his response and I didn't want him to be mad at me. "Do you want to go somewhere else?"

"Nah. I'm just giving you a hard time," he said.

We rambled on, saying nothing of consequence in the easy going manner I had grown accustomed to with him.

"Let's go swimming," Brad suggested suddenly.

"I can't swim," I heard myself say as a wave of fear washed over me. I had not wanted him to know that, but I sure did not want to get in the water with its jellyfish and undertow and stingrays and God-only-knows what else.

"Then let's go get wet," he insisted.

"In there?" I asked jerking my head in the direction of the ocean.

"Of course, in there," he laughed.

"There's all kinds of wiggly things in there. And it's dark!" I added as extra ammunition to my argument.

"Come on. Let's go out to the sand bar. I'll get you out there and back without drowning you."

"Sure! You want me to trust you with my life. What's in

it for me?" I asked. He had already dragged me to the edge of the water, playfully asserting his strength.

I heard a childish whine creep into my voice as I stood with all ten toes planted as firmly as possible in the shifting sand. "Nooooo!" I wailed, startling my cousin into releasing his hold on my arm. He hastened to apologize, and assured me he wouldn't want me to do anything I didn't want to do.

Suddenly, I wanted to go to the sand bar; wanted to more than anything. The mighty ocean was holding me in a grip of fear and embarrassing me in the process. I wouldn't yield to its control. I would never have stepped into its powerful waves alone, but Brad was an expert swimmer and a lifeguard. He planned to study oceanography in college. I knew, realistically, if I were safe with anyone, it was Brad. Blindly, stupidly, I followed him into the watery depths. As my feet left the security of the ocean floor, the thought occurred to me that the first time I volunteered for a drowning it was for a divine purpose, my baptism. This was stupidity!

* * * * *

When Ted's family moved again a short time later, I could count on a letter being in the mailbox almost every day. Some days the mailman brought two or three, all pledging Ted's undying love for me. I only heard what I wanted to hear in his letters. I skimmed over the mushy parts, and focused on the more interesting news. I found comfort in knowing someone cared about me. The long distance relationship was more manageable emotionally than face to face interaction.

One fateful day, I opened a letter from him. Wedged between a description of California's coastline and information on his day to day activities he had written, "I love you and some day I'm going to marry you."

The moment my brain absorbed the message, I felt paralyzed. I did not want to get married. That was the last thing on my mind. But how could I break the news to him? He would be so disappointed. It appeared he already had his mind made up without consulting me. I felt trapped, and I knew that unless Ted changed his mind about marrying me, I would be with him forever. I tried to imagine living with him, and I couldn't.

In desperation, I let my mother read the letter, and asked her what I should do.

"Well, I guess you will have to marry him. You had to have done something to make him fall in love with you. I guess you're stuck with him now."

Never once in my life had she told me I had a choice in anything. My life was run by whatever someone else wanted me to do for them. The prospect of marriage made me ill. I did not answer his letter because I did not know what to say. The inevitable phone call from him came a few days later. He demanded to know what I thought of the idea. I could not hurt his feelings, but I could hedge around the question.

"I can't marry anyone until I finish high school," I told him, "and that's a long way off."

He told me he would wait. Meanwhile, he planned to quit school because he found it boring and a waste of his time.

Vietnam was now a tragic household word and countless numbers of teenage boys were shipping out to frightening destinations like DaNang, Saigon, and CamRhon Bay. Ted seemed determined to join the Army, ordinarily not a bad decision for an eleventh grade drop-out. Considering the heightened condition of the war, however, the timing was less than desirable. Immediately after boot camp, he received orders to depart for Da Nang, South Vietnam, to join a patrol unit in the Mekong Delta.

Despite warnings from everyone I knew, and despite my better judgment, I told Ted I would marry him after I graduated from high school. It was true Ted had no real plans for his future, but I had no real plans for mine either. I figured we would grope our way together. I fostered the false hope that at last a man would take care of me. Only Brad's objection struck a nerve of regret.

"If you love him, I think you should marry him. I just don't think you love him," Brad said as we lingered in his car one night, reluctant to have the evening end.

"How would you know if I love him?" I badgered him.

"Look me in the eye and tell me you love him and I'll believe you," Brad said quietly. I couldn't do that. The unexpected seriousness in his voice caught me off guard. It prevented me from even making eye contact with him. I could feel him looking at me, but I continued to stare straight ahead.

"You're my cousin, Karen, and I care about you. I just hate to see you make a mistake. That's all," he went on.

"And you think I'm making a mistake," I said flatly.

"I don't think you love him. And if you don't, it seems to me you shouldn't marry him," he said matter-of-factly. Damn! Why did he have to put it so simply? It wasn't that cut and dried.

"The plans are already made. I've already told him I would marry him."

"So? You can always tell him you've changed your mind," he said gently. "It's a year away from the wedding date. I thought you wanted to go to college. What happened to those plans?"

"Mamma said she and Daddy had been putting money aside for my college education. She told me in my senior year that Daddy had not put any money into the account like she thought he had. If I go to college, I'll have to work my way through it." I didn't want him to know that crowds and new situations terrified me. Relief that I did not have to meet the challenge of college life neutralized the bitter disappointment of being unable to continue my education.

Brad listened to my explanation before giving his

inevitable advice. "Karen, if you really want to go to college, there's always a way you can go. I'll help you any way I can. Mamma and Daddy would probably let you stay with us and go to college here. But even if you don't go to school, you still don't have to get married."

"Does this mean you don't want to be an attendant at the wedding?" I asked, half afraid of his answer.

"No. If that's what you want to do, I'll do whatever I can to help you be happy. I just don't think you really want marriage right now, and I hope you change your mind."

At seventeen I didn't dare to dream. I felt some unseen force had already determined my life. My marriage had been arranged by someone else, and I was committed to it without benefit of love or any sense of anticipation.

## Chapter Ten
### * * *

We married in Marietta in June of 1967. Ted was assigned to a base on the west coast. California beckoned with a silent promise of adventure and change of lifestyle. We rented a small apartment from an elderly Mexican couple who spoke very little English. Mrs. Ramirez, a tiny Hispanic powerhouse, made it clear she did not usually rent to military families, because they relocated too frequently. However, she took an instant liking to both of us and seemed happy to have us as tenants.

I loved our first apartment with its poinsettia bushes blooming outside the kitchen window, and the gentle evening breezes luring me to explore the neighborhood. Ted repeatedly warned me that it was not safe to wander alone in that part of town, and he worried about me doing that while he was at the base. I laughed at his concern while being held captive by fear of another kind. I could walk the streets alone at night without a hint of worry, but I could not make a phone call or look anyone in the eye without an anxiety attack.

We were newlywed teenagers with very little money and even less self-esteem. Ted needed me in order to feel confident, and I needed him in order to feel wanted. We found some sense of fulfillment with each other and enjoyed married life. California was truly another world away from the old pressures of home, but it was also a lonely place with no money and Ted stuck on the base most of the time.

We moved to San Francisco a few months later. Since affordable housing was not available there, I flew to Alabama to stay with Granny indefinitely. I took an assembly line sewing job at a men's suit factory forty miles away in Columbus, Georgia. Though not exactly my idea of creative design, it was a job I could do as naturally as breathing. I made friends with several girls and lived for breaks and lunch time, the only times allowed for talking. After all, this was a production job and talking cut down on production. That made for a very boring day.

I became an avid clock watcher, partly due to boredom, but mostly because I needed a bathroom break long before they thought we should go. One day I just couldn't wait until the scheduled break time. Mortified, I had to ask my male supervisor for special permission to be excused to the ladies' room. However, once alone in the rest room, I experienced a new and horrible sensation. I could not urinate. Attributing the problem to nervousness, I tried every technique to relax with no success. In pain and embarrassed, I returned to my machine. By lunchtime the pain had increased, making it difficult to walk and impossible to stand straight.

Forced to leave work early, I drove home seeking a sure cure from Granny's capable hands. When a warm bath, hot drinks, and time failed to help, Granny called my aunt for her professional opinion. Being a registered nurse and knowing I was born with only one kidney, Aunt Helen came over to drive me to the doctor's office. The terror of being examined intensified when he sent me straight to the hospital and called a urologist to meet us there. After preliminary tests were completed, they scheduled a cystoscopy and possible surgery.

Over the years, as a result of my father's early sexual abuse, scar tissue had formed in the urethra and finally blocked it completely, making it impossible for me to urinate. Whatever else may have been wrong, I never knew. The doctor did not tell me, and I did not ask. The hospital experience succeeded in removing the scar tissue, but it also drove me backwards in time and left me locked within myself. Unable to eat or sleep, I sat in a fetal position watching wide-eyed with terror whenever a nurse entered the room. My silent tears drove them to compassion.

"I'm sorry," I said to them repeatedly. They were puzzled and wanted to know what I was sorry about. I didn't know. The doctor realized something was wrong beyond my physical ailment. I retreated into myself, unaware of my present reality until I heard the kind voice of a nurse saying, "Your doctor has sent for your husband. He will be here tomorrow night. The Red Cross is arranging for an emergency leave for him."

A thread of comfort brought me back to the real world and helped me cope with a few more days of hospitalization. I counted on Ted to hold me and stabilize my fears. He was counting on the same from me. He found me weak and needy, a shattering blow to his expectations of a few days of rest and relaxation.

Ted secured an extension on his emergency leave, but when time came for him to report to Fort Benning, the nearest military facility, he refused to leave the house. After a few days, Granny worried about legal repercussions and called the chaplain at Fort Benning for advice. He came to talk to Ted who laid in bed, mostly unresponsive to anything that was said to him. The chaplain then called me aside for a long talk. I was still physically weak, and Granny had insisted I not get out of the bed and get dressed just because we expected the chaplain to visit with Ted. We were both surprised when the chaplain asked to speak to me alone. Granny brought me a robe and helped me from the bedroom to her front porch swing. He pulled up a chair and sat across from me.

"I've talked with your husband and tried to reason with

him," he began. "I'm not a psychiatrist, and I don't know what the reason is, but I know he is afraid to return to duty. He says he is concerned about leaving you, but I doubt that is the whole reason. It is more likely he is using you as an excuse to avoid his responsibility. In the military, not showing up for work is a serious infraction. If he does not report today, there will be nothing I can do to help him. If he returns with me I can recommend leniency at his A.W.O.L. hearing, and I will recommend a psychological evaluation and counseling which will help him adjust to military life and afterwards."

I listened without comment while the chaplain filled my ears and head with words whose meanings I did not comprehend. Every sentence filled me with more dread than the one before. "It is up to your husband to decide what to do with this situation," he continued "but my real concern is you. You are much too young to be saddled with this kind of responsibility. I've talked with your grandmother and without knowing you, I know you are a strong young lady with the determination and intelligence to accomplish whatever you want to in life. Have you ever thought of divorcing your husband?"

"No." I wasn't sure I heard him correctly.

"I think you should think about doing just that," he said gently.

I could not have been more surprised if he had slapped me. A man of God recommending divorce? What was this world coming to? "I don't believe in divorce," I told him "and we have only been married a few months."

"That's exactly why you should get out now... before there are any children. You aren't pregnant, are you?" I shook my head. "You are nineteen years old. Don't spend the rest of your life pursuing something that isn't there," he said.

I told myself he meant well, but I suddenly found him presumptuous and his unsolicited advice angered me. Not able to release my frustration through tears, my body began to tremble instead. Granny appeared instantly as if she had been peering through a knothole and ushered me back to bed.

I knew I had to stand by Ted. Here was a military man whom Granny obviously respected telling me I was smart and capable, but Mamma and Daddy had known me longer, and the message they gave me had always been that I was too stupid and undeserving to amount to anything. I didn't want to be "high and mighty" like Mamma accused me of being. I just wanted to be loved by someone, and Ted loved me. I would stick with him, and he would make me happy. What unfair expectations I placed on him! I placed even more on myself. Two children from seriously dysfunctional homes each expecting the other one to make the pain and problems go away.

Eventually the Army released Ted early with an honorable discharge because of my health problems. Miraculously, my kidney behaved itself, and I was able to concentrate on other things.

The National Bank of Fort Benning needed tellers, and Granny knew just the person to contact about hiring me. The bank hired me quickly, and I soon gained an education in banking and in dealing with soldiers. Ted spent the next year lounging at home and dreaming up new excuses why he couldn't get a job. At long last, he decided he could get a job in Indiana where his mother lived. After many arguments and against my better judgment, I gave up a sound job and stable environment and allowed my male-dominated self to follow my unemployed husband as he chased rainbows halfway across the country. Before we settled in, I opened the yellow pages of the phone book and immediately secured a job as a professional babysitter. Ted lacked the sense of urgency I felt about earning a living and was content to live off my income.

Eventually he did go to work for a convenience store, but

he soon found it was not convenient for him! He didn't like working evenings. He didn't like the manager. He didn't like the part of town it was in. After a few weeks he simply did not go in at all. I took on the responsibility of answering the phone when his boss called to see why he was not at work. I made up one excuse after another for him, hoping to keep the company from firing him while trying to reason with Ted. Eventually it became too much for me, and I refused to answer the phone. It rang for hours before the caller gave up and assumed Ted was not coming to work. I knew he would be fired, but I had my own problems I felt incapable of dealing with.

I did not know if I was pregnant and miscarrying or if I was just having some serious cramping after having missed my last menstrual period, but I did know I was giving in to the pain. My nerves were frazzled after two sleepless nights in which visions of hospitals filled my head.

Ted lay on the bed watching television while the phone rang insistently on the nightstand beside him. I had no scheduled babysitting jobs for the next two days and I needed the break. The thought of going to the doctor or hospital brought on anxiety attacks, and at the moment I could think of nothing else.

Surely we must have something for pain around this place, I thought. The kitchen cabinet yielded a bottle of Midol I had bought two years before but never opened, and a bottle half full of aspirin. Which should I take? The thought of swallowing any drug frightened me. Perhaps part of me knew I could not be trusted with such an easy escape tool. Though I never contemplated suicide, I had always wished to fall sleep and not awaken on this earth.

The aspirin I took had not helped an hour later, so I took two Midol and prayed for relief. I was still praying for relief two hours later when I took two more of each. The phone continued to ring, thirty times, then forty. Sleep. Blessed sleep.

Please Lord, just let me go to sleep. I was on the verge of sleep, and highly irritated to be that much out of control and not completely out. I took a few more pills, thinking surely that many would knock me out. Since I never took any type of medication, my body's purified state responded more to the over-the-counter drugs than I anticipated.

Somewhere in the hazy realm between consciousness and oblivion we come face to face with ourselves. As an overwhelming sleep claimed my body, my mind went into action. Questions of eternal value still needed to be settled. What if suicide really was the unpardonable sin as my mother claimed? If I died I would never know the joy of holding my own baby or leaving any accomplishments behind me. No. My curiosity about life got the better of me. I wanted to live, even in all the sadness. And there was incredible sadness. I had more than my share, but not more than I could bear. A thread of hope for a more rewarding life on this earth still lingered.

Trying desperately to say I changed my mind, I garbled something unintelligible to Ted. He was absorbed in a television program and not listening to me. I tried again. Figuring I must be talking in my sleep, he turned the television up louder.

I gave in to the urge to sleep. The next moment of awareness brought with it the frightening realization that this may be my last chance. My mind worked, barely, but my mouth did not. My arms had long since lost any ability to move. I mustered all my strength to form one word. "Pills." I had his attention, but I couldn't explain. I tried again to say I changed my mind. He understood. But would he know what to do? He had always been totally dependent on me. He didn't know how to handle a problem. I heard him talking on the phone to his mother.

The siren annoyed me. I knew people were looking at me but I couldn't see them. I began to throw up. Why didn't I feel better? My eyes hurt. My bladder hurt. Strange voices were saying strange things.

"B.P. dropping!"

"She's conscious!"

They were talking about me! Panic overtook me. At the hospital the police were not satisfied with my solitary answer to their variety of questions which really only asked one thing.

"Why did you take the pills?" one officer asked.

"I wanted to sleep."

"What were you trying to do?" another demanded.

"Were you trying to get attention?"

"I was trying to sleep."

"What is it you want?"

"I want to sleep."

"What were you thinking about before you took the pills?"

"I wanted to go to sleep."

Too angry to be intimidated, I thought it none of their business what I did with my personal life. They were not interested in me as a person, and I was not interested in helping them do their paperwork. I had not hurt anyone else and, therefore, did not consider it anyone's business but my own. They certainly were not of any help to me, and their condescending attitude only made matters worse.

It was January 6, 1970, four days before my twenty-first birthday. I dreaded growing older. What was the point?

I saw no reason to stay in Indiana any longer. Knowing I could stay with Granny again until I got on my feet, I called and told her Ted was not working, and that I was sick. She wired me money to come home immediately. To my dismay, Ted followed me down on the next plane and arrived at Granny's house two hours after I did. I did not have the strength to do anything except let him stay.

My usually reserved grandmother voiced her opinion to

me in private. "You don't have to put up with his shenanigans. You got a place to stay here for as long as you want to." Where had I heard that speech before? It sounded like the same one Granny gave my mother throughout my childhood. I knew my life would be less complicated and happier without Ted in it, but Mamma's "stand by your man" policy never allowed the thought of divorce to enter my mind.

Mamma had recently bought a small rental house in Atlanta and it was vacant at that time. We rented it from her and I began working at a corporate office in town.

There I met Alex, who became my friend, my lover, and almost my husband. Alex worked in a different department, but our paths crossed every morning. Since we both went to lunch at the same time, he asked me to go to lunch with him sometimes. I talked with Ted about it, and he had no objection. Alex was also married, and the four of us soon became friends. Ted enjoyed the finer things in life and Alex certainly had them. He very much enjoyed Alex's ski boat, lavish entertainment, and classic cars. I was drawn to other qualities in him.

An accountant by profession, Alex's life exuded the organization that was lacking in mine. His mathematical mind had a simple, concise way of looking at life that added logic to my cluttered confusion.

Ted still refused to work, and although he seemed to think the world of me, he treated me with disrespect and gave me no support of any kind. Alex took notice of each cutting remark and each act of unacceptable behavior.

"Why do you let him treat you the way he does?" he asked me one evening when we had a moment alone.

Except for being perpetually unemployed, I thought all men treated women the way Ted treated me. Compared to my father, Ted treated me very well. He never hit me and I had complete freedom to do anything I wanted to do. Over time, I did see a clear difference in the way Alex treated me and how

Ted responded to me.

Alex pampered me and treated me with tenderness. Eventually, I did respond to my human need for compassion, protection, and love. I thrived on his attention. He wanted me to marry him, quit working, fulfill my desire to go to college, and do only those things I wanted to do for a while.

His was a marriage of convenience, and although he shared my religious upbringing and convictions of fidelity, he also needed happiness. After many tears and much soul searching, we told our spouses of our intentions. His wife was self-supporting and self-sufficient enough to handle the shock, but Ted was close to suicidal.

My feelings of having to take care of his feelings were too deeply ingrained. In addition, the overriding conviction that it was just plain wrong to destroy two marriages to create a third haunted me day and night. My life with Ted was nothing short of misery, but I wasn't sure I could live with myself if I left him for Alex. Somewhere in the darkened tunnels of my heart and soul, I knew if my marriage with Ted ended it must be because it ended on its own, unhampered by outside interference. I backed out of my agreement to marry Alex, and he and his wife remained together. However, my relationship with him continued off and on secretly for the next twenty years.

## Chapter Eleven

*** 

I worried alternately about getting pregnant and not getting pregnant. The idea of my body changing beyond my control was unthinkable. So was the idea of never being a mother. I had so much love to give, but no desire to produce a miniature me. I felt that anything I could create would only be a disaster. It would be a boy for sure, and it would grow up to be like my father or my brothers, and I would hate him. If I had the good grace to have a girl, then she would surely inherit my acne and my shyness, and she would hate me for it.

I used nothing for birth control, but when I missed a cycle I pretended I had not. I painfully accepted the conclusion that I was not ever going to be psychologically able to handle being pregnant and giving birth. That left the much more difficult process of adoption as my only option for motherhood. That decision was not a secondhand one, since I had always wanted to adopt two children, but it meant I could fulfill only half my dreams.

I began writing to doctors, missionaries overseas, adoption agencies, lawyers, and friends in other states. I pursued any avenue that might possibly lead to a baby. Ted never objected to whatever I wanted to do, but he still did not have a regular job, and I knew we would never be given a child under those conditions. I worried and prayed and prodded him to get a job. The Vietnamese orphans tore at my heart. Reports of orphanages being bombed and children being torn apart by the horrors of that war flooded the news. We applied with an agency that handled overseas adoptions. We had decided to adopt a Vietnamese child, when I heard about a woman due to deliver in seven months who planned to place the child for adoption. We decided on the local adoption. I wanted the baby so desperately, I gave Ted an ultimatum: Get a job or get out.

Ted became more responsible and seemed to have a reason to go to work. We had to come up with thousands of dollars for the medical and legal expenses. It seemed the seven months would never pass, but the most exciting day of my life finally arrived.

Our attorney, John, and his secretary picked our newborn daughter up at the hospital and brought her to us at his office. His secretary laid her in my arms, and I folded the blanket away from her tiny face to see her better. "She has her thumb in her mouth!" I stared in awe. I had never seen a newborn sucking its thumb.

"Oh, yes," John said as if suddenly remembering an old message. "She's an old pro at that. The doctor said when he tried to suction her throat at birth, she kept putting her thumb back in her mouth."

We all stood around her wanting a better look. I all but stripped her naked checking her out. Not only was she healthy and beautiful, but smart. We could tell that at four days old. If her thumb fell out of her mouth, she would locate her nose with the palm of her hand, then slide her thumb into her mouth. Then she would use her other hand to hold that one in place.

"The head nurse said to warn you she's spoiled already, that she's a good baby but she likes to be held," John continued to remember little things he was supposed to tell me.

We stopped at Ted's office to show her off. For five years we had dreamed and planned and waited for her. Our close friends had shared our waiting game. It would be unthinkable to go home without going by the Jones' house first. They were waiting with open arms to hold my first baby. Angela Jill arrived on this earth with two extra sets of doting "grandparents". Besides Mr. and Mrs. Jones, "Granny Ruby" and "Grandpa Mick" soon grew so attached to her that a weekly visit was a must. Phone reports were a daily routine. Together we watched her grow. She thrived on the encouragement and love of those older adults who applauded each new achievement and performance in her life. Ruby and Mick were friends we had come to love in the two short years we had known them. I thought of how much stability my grandmother gave to my early years, and I prayed that these people so dear and precious to me would fill whatever gaps I might leave in developing Angela's character.

The nurses were right about her being good. She was so good, I worried about her. She never cried even when I knew she was hungry. Wet diapers didn't bother her. She slept at least four hours at a time during the night, awakened for her bottle, and immediately fell asleep for another long stretch of time. I spent the next two months in utter fascination. I was the typical silly first-time mother thinking mine was the first child to ever follow a moving object with her eye or smile when Mommy's face came into her line of vision. It soon became obvious we would not be able to live on Ted's income alone. Regrettably, I returned to work.

There was really nothing new to learn since I had worked there several months earlier. The first few days were spent trying to fit in at the new branch office. I had just decided that my current co-workers were either a bunch of snobs, or I didn't possess whatever it takes to make new friends, when the blonde named Kelly who worked the station next to mine decided to introduce herself. We made small talk and I discovered she and her husband, Tom, had just moved to our area from another state, and she was trying to get pregnant.

Before the end of the week Kelly invited us over for supper, saying they had not met very many friends yet, and they would like to get to know us better. Suspicion nagged me, forcing me to reconcile my policy of not trusting people until they proved themselves with my desire to have friends. She was inviting us into her home, and though I had reservations, I accepted immediately. It never occurred to me to ask Ted first. He may complain and almost always did, but he would do whatever I decided anyway. His refusal to go caught me by surprise. We bickered over it until time to go out the door. I dressed Angela and packed what she would need for the evening. Only when we were preparing to get in the car did Ted grudgingly decide that he had nothing to do anyway, so he might as well go along.

The evening progressed smoothly as Kelly and I carried the conversation from one subject to another. The men gave new meaning to the term "small talk", never exchanging more than a handful of words all night. Alone afterwards, Tom lamented to Kelly, "Karen is okay but Ted is the most boring person I've ever met in my life."

I was enduring more of the same from Ted. "Do me a favor," he said. "Don't ever ask me to go to those people's house again."

Kelly and I ignored them both and formed our own relationship. Kelly was fascinated with my precious daughter and couldn't wait to have one of her own. Angela completely absorbed me. I spent most of my time, money, and energy on her. Naturally, I liked anyone who showed interest in her. When Angela was five months old, I gave Kelly a ride to her appointment with her gynecologist. This time was different. She came out with the news written all over her face. I said, "You're pregnant!" That was the bond that clinched our friendship - two new moms planning our babies' futures. Our husbands followed suit and we all began doing things together and became friends.

It was Kelly who told me a month later that our

supervisor wanted to see me in her office. Even though I knew I had done nothing wrong, I was sick with worry. Sure I was going to be fired, I immediately reacted with a furious feeling of frustration over all the unfairness in the world. I gathered from the look on Kelly's face that I was in deep trouble. Trembling, I stepped into my supervisor's office. She looked me in the face and said, "I'm sorry to tell you this, Karen, but I received a phone call just a few minutes ago. Your father died this morning." She added kindly, "You can use my office if you would like to be alone for a few minutes."

"No! No, I... I... just thought you were going to say something else," I answered. I was breathing heavily, not quite knowing how to adjust to this absolutely wonderful news. I knew she took my reaction as grief, and I knew to keep pretending. It was hard to do since I wanted to dance around the room.

I had not told anyone Daddy had been in a coma now for nine days, and that he was only forty nine years old. I had not told anyone he was sick, for that matter. I had been expecting him to die, but nothing prepared me for the exultation I felt. He would never be a threat to my little daughter! I felt as though I had been given a new lease on life. I went to his funeral, out of respect for my mother. Personally, I considered it an interruption to my life, and I rejoiced that it would be the last time he could summon me to his side.

I used the funeral as a chance to visit with friends and relatives. Mamma and Daddy had moved to Alabama a few years before, and they were living there when he died. It had been a long time since I had seen Robin; much too long. I could not seem to get on the same wave length with her. She was clearly happy to see me, but so much tension and anger hung in the air. I was disturbed by our visit.

November came and went, and I suffered from a flu-like illness from Thanksgiving through Christmas and into January.

Several people told me I must be pregnant, but I knew I couldn't be. I took birth control pills every morning and pregnancy couldn't possibly make me this sick. I lost weight and dehydrated. When I was no longer able to go to work and had to ask my mother to move in temporarily to feed and care for Angela, I knew I had to consult a doctor. When he confirmed the pregnancy, I fell apart at the seams.

I didn't want to be pregnant. I had an eight-month-old daughter, a decent job, and before I became pregnant, my health. I listened to the doctor's recommendation about being under a urologist's care for the duration of the pregnancy and spending the last two or three months in the hospital as a precaution against my one kidney failing. I looked at the X-rays showing the misplaced organ and the stress a pregnancy in its final stages would place on it, and I knew what I must do.

I tried to talk to Ted about it, but his only comment was, "It's your decision." My doctor's only comment was, "I don't believe in abortion, but I will perform it if that is your decision." He softened his remark by adding, "If you decide on that, you must look at it as a therapeutic abortion."

So the doctor and I decided to perform an abortion the following week. My mother agreed to take care of Angela. The only "counseling" I received came from her as we left the house at 5:30 the morning of the surgery. Vomiting as usual and shaking from fear and a multitude of other emotions, I heard my mother warn me in her best authoritarian voice, "God will get you for this young lady. He just might decide to take that other baby in there away from you if you get rid of this one. You better think about what you are doing!"

Didn't she understand? Didn't anyone understand that I couldn't think? I wanted someone else to do the thinking. I couldn't gather information, process it, and make a logical decision when I couldn't even hold my head up. I needed someone to comfort me, reassure me, understand me, care about me.

Ted drove, and I cried silently all the way to the hospital. In the parking lot, I sat frozen in my seat, unable to walk that final lap of the journey into the hospital. Ted's impatience with my emotionalism showed. Zombie-like, I slowly opened the car door and walked unknowingly into one of the worst experiences of my life.

Ted left me with a nurse so he could take care of the paperwork. She directed me to a room with rows of dressing chambers and handed me a surgical gown to change into. "Are you all right?" she asked, noticing the tributaries of tears on my face. I nodded, unable to speak. She returned a few minutes later and found me as she had left me, sitting on the bench with the privacy curtain still open. I had not even removed my shoes, but sat staring at them in horror as though they had somehow betrayed me by bringing me there. I had given up trying to control the shaking which caused my teeth to chatter, concentrating instead on clenching them together.

She tried to assess the situation and my condition. "Do you need some help getting undressed?" I shook my head vehemently, at the same time drawing my knees up to my chest and scrunching into a corner on the narrow bench.

"Are you having pain anywhere?" No answer from me. "Is it too cold in here for you?" She paused. "Would you like for me to bring your husband in here?" Still no response from me. The concern and kindness in her voice attempted to reassure me. I wanted to thank her, but I dared not trust myself to form words. I could not even look at her.

She's going to get impatient. Say something! I chided myself. I was convinced that once she became impatient, she would slap me and then it would be so much worse. I was once again three years old, abandoned and traumatized in a hospital room. I was frozen in fear, a typical survival response for someone enduring post traumatic stress, even years after the

137

event.

"I'll go get your doctor, sweetie," she said.

"No!" I gasped and then sobbed uncontrollably.

She knelt down, asking if I wanted her to stay with me. "Please," I begged between sobs. I needed someone I could trust, and I felt safer with her than Ted - safer with a total stranger with a kind voice than with anyone I knew.

She kept talking, allowing me to keep silent. She explained step by step what would be done, emphasizing the comforting things I would encounter.

In the operating room, the anesthesiologist deadened the area for the I.V. as I had requested. Even so, it felt as if he were boring a hole through my hand when he inserted the needle. I made a low growling noise when I could stand it no longer.

"Are you still with me?" he asked when he was finally finished.

"Barely," I said.

"Your veins are very elastic. That makes it tough to get the needle in correctly. No wonder you don't like I.V.'s. Without the xylocain it really would have been rough."

"You are the first person who ever believed me."

"Oh, I believe you. I always believe in a patient's pain. The good part is it's all over now. Let me round up your doctor and this will all be over before you know it." He left me alone for a few minutes and I immediately lost what little composure I had. When had someone fastened two belts across my body that held me to this table? And who did it? The anesthesiologist returned momentarily to find me hyperventilating, vomiting, and sobbing noisily.

This scene forced my doctor to do a quick role change from gynecologist to psychologist. He knew nothing of my past and next to nothing about my present life. Gently, he questioned me, probing to find a reason for my strange behavior. I didn't tell him about being tied to the bed while my father raped me. I didn't tell him about the cigarette burns or the rags stuffed in my mouth, or the brainwashing, or the terror of wondering what was going to happen next. I didn't even realize how similar being at the doctor's mercy was like being at my father's mercy. But the fear and the feeling of helplessness were the same.

"I just don't want this operation, but I have to," I finally lamented by way of explanation.

"No. You don't have to. It's not too late to change your mind. Do you want to think about it some more? We can always reschedule," he said.

Ted would be furious. "No. I don't have any choice. I can't keep being sick all the time and I couldn't go through this again." I burst into tears.

Dr. Harmon nodded to the man in charge of putting me to sleep. "Let's get this over with for her." He continued to stroke my hair and talk to me until the other doctor cleared his throat. I opened my eyes to see him shaking his head.

"Her vital signs have to stabilize first."

"Karen, what is it you're afraid of?" Dr. Harmon asked. I did not tell him I was afraid of going to hell for this, afraid my baby daughter would die because of my sin, and afraid I was giving up my only chance to ever give birth, and that I was carrying a tremendous load of guilt for murdering a child that never had a chance.

The real problem lay wrapped in the rags of immobilizing terror of being in a hospital at the mercy of men sticking things up my vagina and looking at my body. He sat against the narrow edge of the gurney, facing me. He assured me it was a simple procedure. It would be over soon. I would be home in a few hours, and I could still change my mind.

I remained calm in the recovery room only because I knew I would be going home as soon as I could sit up. My first waking thought brought the awareness that I was not sick to my stomach anymore. For the first time in three months I didn't feel like I had the flu. I felt wonderful!

A few days later, Mamma called from Eufaula to tell me Robin was dead and to give me information on funeral arrangements.

"What do you mean, she's dead?" I asked as a protective numbness steeled my emotions against her assaulting words.

"She shot herself with a hunting rifle. Put the barrel of the gun in her mouth and pulled the trigger with her toe." Mamma said this new information as though giving me a grocery list.

I did not go to the funeral, and I did not really grieve for my friend until many years later. I did not know how to deal with her death, so I ignored that it had occurred. I also put the abortion and my childhood behind me. I focused entirely on my new phase of life. I quit my job and stayed home with Angela. I feared losing her so much, I decided that if anything should happen to her I would be with her when it did.

Angela was ten months old when Tom and Kelly's firstborn arrived on the scene. I saw Kelly briefly as they wheeled her from the delivery room to her room. Shaking from excitement and the epidural, she couldn't quit talking about baby Cierra. Life was just about perfect.

Then when Cierra was six months old, Tom's job required them to relocate to Texas. I couldn't blame them for their decision to move so far away, but I missed them before they ever left. We wrote to each other often, and when we were especially homesick for each other, we would call and talk for hours. We exchanged pictures of the kids and made plans for our next visit together.

# Chapter Twelve
## * * *

I alternated between babysitting and making wedding dresses to supplement our income. Angela was such a good baby, I always wanted to be with her. As she grew older I knew she needed other children to play with, and she needed time away from me.

I determined she should have all the benefits I never had. A constant awareness of my phobias and the effects they could have on my child compelled me toward a conscious effort to counteract them. Though I was terrified of the dentist and never went myself, I had Ted take Angela to the dentist before she was three and continued to do so every six months. I wanted more than anything to spare her the fear and pain, at least the needless fear and pain, that would keep her from enjoying life.

I searched diligently for a pediatrician I felt to be worthy of treating my child. He was located 30 miles from our house, but the drive, when necessary, was worth every mile.

Angela learned to swim at the age of four and enjoyed the water so much I envied her aquatic adventures. Though still terrified of water myself, I gave in to her pleas to "get in the pool with me". I acclimated myself little by little, first sitting on the steps, then standing and leaning against the edge. Through sheer determination, I eventually taught myself to swim; not well enough to save my life, but enough to enjoy the shallow end of the pool.

We began attending church more regularly and I taught Sunday School. I served on the preschool committee. Getting involved helped me pretend I was normal, and that helped drive my childhood completely out of my consciousness.

By the time Angela turned five, I had started doing childcare in my home on a full-time basis. I made a conscious choice to remain in my profession. For here, sheltered from the business world of male authority figures, I had control. Business dealings were handled with mothers for the most part, and they were grateful for my services.

It helped that I liked children, but that was not the driving force behind my decision. Though I had been fortunate in finding two good sitters for Angela when I worked outside the home, I was distrustful of leaving her with anyone. I needed to know every minute of every day and night that she was safe and happy. There also existed an even more urgent, though not as recognizable, need to protect myself from the predators, both real and imagined, in the workplace.

Locked inside my own home in the safe, smiling world of children, I could function quite normally. No one, including myself, would be likely to spot the neurotic behavior so cleverly disguised. I was operating my own business, staying home with my child, and making six sets of parents happy. I was also hiding from the outside world, afraid to let go of my child, and being terribly used at times.

Mamma urged me to get a real job. So did Ted. A subtle stigma attached to child care providers implied that a woman could not do anything else in life if she resorted to keeping kids (part of the long-standing devaluation of children). Working at an office was more glamorous by comparison. Only Granny urged me to do what made me happy. Angela made me happy. Beyond that I had no idea of what I wanted to be when I grew up.

* * * * *

The safe, smiling world of children could not protect me from all things. The day finally came when I could avoid doctors no longer. The old problem of not being able to urinate returned. Over a period of days, I tried everything from prayer to self-catherization. Pain forced me to take a few days off work. The condition eventually developed into uremia despite my best efforts. I lay in my own vomit on the kitchen floor, fighting a ferocious headache along with the pain from an extended bladder. Although the thought of my precious little girl being left motherless grieved me, rationale could not counteract the fear of repeating a hospital experience. I knew what I *should* do, but I was limited in what I *could* do. I no longer prayed to live. I prayed to die.

Ted stood above me condemning my behavior, threatening to call an ambulance, reminding me of my obligations to him, and wallowing in his own inadequacies of not knowing what to do. Eventually the pain forced me to get help. I asked Ted to call our preacher who came to the house. The pastor did not know how to handle the emotional crisis, but he did know it was a life and death emergency and something must be done. He questioned me until, in desperation, I revealed the truth about my father. He asked if there was any doctor I could trust at all. I mentioned my gynecologist. I did not tell him about the abortion four years earlier, the memory of which was still too fresh on my mind.

"Karen, what if I contact your doctor on your behalf, explaining your fears and the situation. He can help you. Someday you will have to deal with your past before it costs you your life, but right now you have to get some relief."

"He's a gynecologist. He can't help me," I cried.

"It's a start. If this doctor is as kind as you say he is, he will find a caring urologist for you."

In the doctor's office, I begged him to be the only

143

physician to look at my body.

"I'm trying to figure out a way to do that," he said. "If I am your primary doctor, I have to have some reason for admitting you that I am responsible for, and the real problem is out of my field."

"Do a tubal ligation. Cut off a breast. I don't care what you do. I don't care if I live or die, just don't make me see another doctor while I'm awake."

And so, thanks to the miracle worker in the white coat, the scar tissue was cauterized from my bladder by a urologist he called in, and the fear of pregnancy was eliminated at the same time. In the recovery room, he renigged on his promise to let me go home as soon as I could sit up.

"I know I promised you would not have to stay overnight, but we are giving you the maximum amount of morphine and you are still in pain. We can't send morphine home with you. You can still go home if you want to, but I'm afraid you will just end up back in the emergency room and that would be even more traumatic for you. What would make it easier for you to spend the night here, just for one night?"

I wanted to rock back and forth in a fetal position, stare straight ahead, and pretend he wasn't there, but the slightest movement caused the rubber catheter to rub against burned skin inside the urethra, so I was forced to deal with the problem in a more mature fashion. I did not know what would make it easier, but with his helpful suggestions, it was decided that Ted would stay overnight with me, no one would enter my room except one particular nurse, and she would administer pain medication but would not touch me without my permission.

When the doctor came to dismiss me the next day, he asked Ted to step outside and he said to me, "When you've recovered physically, you need to tell your husband about your past. This is not a burden you should carry all by yourself. I can help you find a good counselor, if you like. But you need someone who can help you sort through all that pain and guilt you've been carrying around all these years."

I nodded, hugged my bottle of Percocet, and disregarded everything he said. I left the hospital with a catheter in my bladder, a bottle of antibiotics in my hand, and morphine in my blood.

After ten minutes of stony silence on the ride home from the hospital, Ted insisted that he be informed of whatever I had told the preacher and the doctor "behind his back".

Had it not been for a medical emergency, the one thing in life I could not handle on my own, I don't know if I ever would have revealed my secret to my husband. I didn't feel ready to tell him. Like so many things in my life, I felt forced to comply. Still, as I thought of a way to say what must be said, I found myself anticipating a new understanding from him. Surely he would see how difficult life was for me and find a new admiration and respect for me.

The car seemed to hit every rough spot in the pavement, and the ride brought agony to my midsection. Yet, the physical pain somehow made it easier to tell Ted the plain facts without worrying about how it was worded. He stared straight ahead for a long time before breaking the silence.

"Why didn't you tell anyone what was going on with your father while it was going on?"

"I was little. I didn't know how to tell."

"Well, I can understand when you were 3, 4, or 5, but when you were older you should have done something about it; certainly by the time you were a teenager."

I bristled with righteous indignation. Words would only fall on deaf ears, and, as much as I wanted him to understand, I knew he never would. Instead of gaining a new appreciation for me, he valued me even less. My relationship with Ted worsened after this disclosure, but my relationship with myself reached a turning point. In exposing the secret, I freed myself to be honest, and, in being honest, I freed myself to heal.

In verbally defending myself to Ted, I clarified for myself that I was not to blame, but was an innocent victim of a powerful man and a powerful system. Granny had always said, "Be true to yourself Katie, and don't expect too much from other people." I never knew quite what that meant, but I was beginning to.

I never mentioned the subject again to my husband, just as I never mentioned it to my mother, and for the same reasons. There were both too self-centered to care about my issues. I felt that I would not be validated or supported by any member of my family with the possible exception of my grandmother. I thought she would believe me and stand beside me, but I was not willing to take that chance. Besides, she was old and not in good health.

I ignored my doctor's advice to find a counselor for two reasons. My mother always said, "Counseling is a tool of the devil", so I was afraid of the only tool that could have helped me.

Secondly, despite the doctor's extraordinary care and concern during my hospital stay, I still heard his advice to get help as criticism. No matter what words he used or what tone of voice delivered the message, I would have heard, "You are a sick person. You are not a fit wife or mother. You are shameful. You are dirty. You're not smart enough or good enough to handle things on your own. You need someone to tell you how to live your life."

In my ignorance, I suspected counseling to be more like hypnosis. I thought counseling would control me and tell me what to do rather than enable me to control my own life. If I had only known then that it would open up options for me and show me how to make better choices, I would have sought help right away. Telling was a difficult, courageous step toward recovery, even though it was dragged out of me. That all-important step demanded a supportive audience and the people in my family were hostile members on the side of secrecy. I did not know there was an outside support system of other survivors, therapists, etc. so I did the worst thing possible. I packed the secret away into a dark area of my heart, and left it there to fester another seven years.

Breaking the code of silence had benefited me in some ways. My pastor had done his part to help. My doctor had not only saved my life, but guarded my psychological well-being. Still, my trust factor was so low, I ran like a wounded, scared rabbit to the safety of my home and familiar routine.

* * * * *

Granny had broken her hip the year before, but recovered by sheer willpower. Now eighty-four, she had been complaining of her back hurting for several months. I visited her whenever possible. Freeways had cut travel time from our house to hers to about three and a half hours. Still, it was a long trip, and gasoline was expensive.

I wanted to bring Granny to our house to stay for a few months, but her independent spirit forbade it. She wanted her own house and her own things surrounding her. Eventually, she began spitting up blood and had trouble breathing. Mamma called me and asked what to do. I could not stand the thought of Granny not being able to breathe. She said Granny did not want to go to the hospital. She wanted to die at home. I told Mama I thought she should take her to the hospital anyway, a decision I would regret forever. I thought going to the hospital would relieve her pain. It only prolonged it.

When I went to her room to visit her, she begged to see Angela. Five-year-olds were not allowed in patients' rooms, even if that was the patient's dying request. I sneaked Angela up the back stairway and into Granny's room without the nurses knowing. Afterwards, when I sat alone with my grandmother, she called me closer to her side. Twisting in pain,

147

she said, "Sugar, I don't want to go off and leave ya'll, but it looks like that's what I'm gone haf to do if I'm ever gone get easy."

I held her hand and kissed her head as I talked to her. "Granny, don't you worry about any of us. All we want is for you to quit hurting. You know we love you and it kills me to see you in this much pain."

I had to get away from the hospital. Torn between leaving her alone and having to endure the hospital scene any longer, I left, promising to be back the next weekend.

A few days later while Angela attended kindergarten and I made lunch for the day care children, the phone rang.

"Hello."

"Karen." As soon as I heard my mother speak, I knew the end had come. "She's gone." Her voice wavered and broke on the last word.

"I'll be there as soon as I can get away," I said. Part of me wanted to ask if she suffered in her final moments, but another part of me was afraid to know.

I hung up the phone, trying to comprehend this new knowledge. Granny no longer lived on this earth. Even as I made preparations to drive to Alabama to help make final arrangements, I caught myself packing things she might enjoy.

The cold December wind lashed against my body but was no match for the hard freeze that paralyzed my heart. I stood on the steps outside the funeral home trying to prepare myself for seeing Granny in her coffin. I had seen her in pain, thrashing and fighting the invisible demon inside her body. I had seen her wearing contentment, luxuriating in the feel and smell of her infant grandchild in her lap. I could remember seeing disappointment, anger, fear, joy, and sorrow on her beloved face. Over the years I had seen my grandmother every way imaginable. Except dead. Only in cold reality could I see her that way, and I could not prepare myself for that raw confrontation. I was no stranger to funeral homes. I had said farewell to many people, but never to one I loved this much.

My heart waged war with my brain. My brain said, "This is the natural order of things, and at least she is not suffering anymore."

My heart screamed back, "I don't care if she lived a long, full life. It still isn't fair. She's too good to be dead. She should be immortal. Why don't the bad people die instead?"

Brain ultimately won the battle. "You have to do what you have to do," it said.

I knew that was so. If they don't have her bun fixed right, I will redo it myself, I resolved silently as I turned and marched through the door.

The first look was so much worse than I thought it would be. This frail body with its gray hair perfectly coiled at the back of the head looked exactly like my Granny... except it was not breathing. It is true that grief is the most selfish of passions. If I could have thrown myself over her and breathed life back into her, I would have. Even if it meant her twisting in pain, and moaning, "Jesus, help me!"

I wanted to touch her beautiful old face and kiss her forehead, but I knew I could not handle the cold rock-hardness where softness and warmth had always been. I swallowed hard, wiped away an escaping tear, and walked away to examine the flowers. They reminded me of all the chrysanthemums, daffodils, and dahlias Granny had planted to spruce up her sparce yard. I smiled to myself, but the smile turned downward, threatening to betray my outward calm.

She didn't belong in this strange place with its melancholy background music. Did all funeral parlors play that stuff? I never noticed before. It was supposed to be soothing, but it wasn't Granny's style. Nor mine. She would have preferred the hum of human voices, and laughter, and people to feel at home when they came to see her. We brought her home to stay overnight before the burial. Her house lacked sufficient heat to accommodate all the friends who would be coming by, so we decided to use my mother's house next door for the wake. It wasn't home to Granny, but it was close enough, far better than the funeral home.

Someone placed the arrangement I bought next to the head of the coffin. The flowers were arranged atop a piece of styrofoam shaped like an open Bible. A toy telephone perched on the Bible with the receiver dangling. It read, "Jesus called. Granny answered." It proved to be more of a comfort to me than for the grandchildren and great-grandchildren for whom I ordered it.

Friends gathered and stayed for hours. Many stayed overnight talking about Miss Ginny. I listened carefully, drinking in these tidbits of trivia. I learned rare and precious facts about her that night. It amazed me how many men respected her knowledge of masculine subjects like plowing and roofing and working on cars. They all remembered a time when Miss Ginny had shown them how to do something better or fix something they had all given up on.

She must have been something of a rebel in her time. It amused me to find she wore overalls way back when that was not the accepted thing to do. I had never seen her in anything but a dress with the exception of the one time we talked her into wearing a bathing suit into the ocean. I found it almost as hard to imagine her in overalls as it had been to imagine her sweet face in a casket. A gentleman about twenty years her junior had the room captivated recounting a story about the only time he saw her wearing Grandaddy's pants.

"I stopped by one day and found Langston on the front porch drunk," he said. "Miss Ginny was out in the field plowing. Well, I had some important information they needed to know, and I knew Langston would never know I came by, much less give a message straight. So I went on out to the field. Now I had heard she could plow as good as any man, but I'd never seen her doing it. She saw me coming and stopped the mule. She pulled out a hanky from her pocket and wiped her face. I was so surprised I said to her, 'Miss Ginny, is that Langston's overalls you wearing?' 'Yessir, I believe they are,' she said. I looked at her and I says to her, 'But Miss Ginny, I can't believe my eyes. You're out here in overalls!' She laughed then and she asked me what I wore when I plowed. I told her, 'overalls.' Then she says to me, 'All right then, Dudley. When I see you plowin' in a dress, I'll wear a dress to plow my field.' I felt like a school boy that didn't have a lick of sense. It sure put me in my place. I never questioned anything she did after that. I just figured she had a good reason for whatever it might be."

"It's a good thing you didn't show up on a different occasion she told me about once," a lady next to me said with a twinkle in her eye. "Miss Ginny was plowing near the creek when something ran up her pant leg. She was afraid it might be a snake, so she grabbed a handful of material and crushed it in her fist. Then she proceeded to strip the overalls off right where she stood. It was only a lizard, but the overalls were no longer wearable. She said she walked back to the house in her underwear and shirt, hoping she didn't pass the preacher cutting through the path from his house to the church."

I gathered that Langston stayed drunk a lot and she took care of anything that needed attention. Yet I never heard that from Granny. Only once did she ever mention him being drunk. Around the age of twelve, I was sitting in front of the fireplace while she stoked the fire. One of my little cousins made a comment about how much it would hurt if you got burned by that fire poker. She laughed one of her rare, hearty laughs and said, "Langston could tell you that if he was still alive. It wasn't funny at the time, but now that I recollect it, it strikes me funny."

"Tell us what happened, Granny," we begged. It seems

that Grandpa got fresh with her one night while in a drunken state and would not take "no" for an answer. She warned him to stay away from her 'til he sobered up if he didn't want a hot fire poker up side of his face. She claimed he was a lot more respectful of her after that night. I was beginning to understand why I knew so little about him. They all lived by the creed "If you can't say something good about someone, don't say anything at all." I didn't think I would have liked him very much, and I wondered if he was as bad as my father.

Granny had made a lot of friends in eighty-four years, but most of them her age had passed from this life before her. I looked around at all the people whose lives had been touched by hers. No doubt all of them had eaten vegetables from her garden at one time or another. All of them had rocked in her porch swing or sat on the front steps and passed the time of day with her. I wished I could know everything they knew about her. Everyone had different memories of her it seemed, yet they all shared some of the same ones. Everything she did in life filtered through the fingers of love.

"She ain't gone far," some older lady said. "Every time I pass by her place I'm still gonna see Miss Ginny sittin' in that old rocker waving at me."

"Why every time I make corn bread dumplin's, I remember the day she showed me how," another lady chimed in.

"You know, most ever Sunday mornin' while I'm awaitin' for services to begin, I sit in that pew and I think about when we used to hold services in Miz Ginny's kitchen. Those were some good times," an elderly gentleman said pensively, leaning over his cane.

She was living through these people, I realized. I thought of how many ways I copied her behavior, lifestyle, and habits. Surely as long as I lived she would be so much a part of me.

Her funeral service was held in the very church she helped

start. No longer a tent or a one-room clapboard structure, the three-story brick building's steeple reached for the sky. It had been four years since Granny entered this sanctuary. She had found it quite a chore to get up those many steps for her eightieth birthday celebration, given by her family and the congregation she loved. Now with tears and sadness, six pall bearers carried her into the church for the last time. Her body was laid to rest next to her husband's in the Eufaula Cemetery, but her spirit and her memory would never be laid to rest.

# Chapter Thirteen
## * * *

A year later Kelly and Tom moved back to our area with their two children, a brand new daughter named Heather and Cierra who was now five years old. They rented a hotel suite just around the corner from us while they searched for a house to buy. That arrangement turned out to be opportunistic for all of us. Ted and I were going through the adoption process once more. Having trusted friends nearby as a sounding board helped, and I was thrilled to have them in town to share the excitement with us. A few weeks later our second daughter entered our lives.

The attorneys told us to expect an infant from a Latin American birth mother and a Caucasian birth father. However, the pediatrician who delivered the baby said she appeared darker than he expected and there was a strong possibility the father was black. It is true that if we had known from the beginning to expect a child of a black parent we may have done more soul-searching before deciding to adopt her. I would have still wanted her for my daughter from a personal standpoint, but we did not handle social prejudice very well, and even in the late 1970's, a white family with a black child was not accepted in society. A wise person would consider all that.

At this point, however, none of that mattered. I had loved her since she was an idea in my head, since she first appeared as a spark of hope in my heart six weeks earlier. She was the answer to many prayers and the color of her skin did not change that. It turned out that both bits of information about the father were incorrect. His contribution of Mexican lineage made Maria a full-blooded, beautiful Hispanic baby. The experience revealed valuable insight to me about myself and about our culture. Love doesn't have a color. Any child might have been my child, and in a sense every child belongs to all of us. Maria, with her shining black eyes and hair as soft as down, was a sweet culmination of my lifelong dreams.

Tom and Kelly bought a rambling farm house on five acres of land just south of Atlanta. We lived only four miles from them inside the city limits. Kelly and I couldn't believe our good luck. Maria was two months younger than Heather. With our daughters so close in age, Kelly decided not to return to the business world, but to do childcare also. She hired an employee and opened a group daycare home with a licensed capacity of twelve. We found excuses to see each other almost every day. The babies learned to walk and talk and shared everything from toys and clothes to germs and bad habits. Heather taught Maria to scream and open dresser drawers. In return, Maria taught her to stick things up her nose and unfasten her seat belt. Kelly called them salt and pepper in reference to the contrast of Heather's cotton white hair against the silky blackness of Maria's.

In the summer of 1981, Ted was out of town on business. One evening after I gave my girls their supper and put them to bed, I called Kelly and told her I felt very ill but was not going to the hospital. She understood the depth of my phobia and knew it was pointless to try to reason with me. I asked her to check on my kids the next morning in case I was not able to care for them. Worried, she called me several times during the night. Sometimes she found me complaining that my head hurt, and sometimes she found me disoriented and unaware of who she was or my own identity.

Kelly was correct in her suspicion of meningitis. Fortunately, it was viral and not bacterial. I could not cope with the trauma of hospitalization. Mercifully, another personality moved in to rescue me. A personality, I learned later, who was not as nice as I. I could not recall going to the hospital or coming home, and I could remember only three brief moments from my five-day stay. The other personality prevented the doctors and hospital staff from doing any tests on me, a feat I would have been powerless to accomplish.

I left the hospital with my halo tarnished and my name on the top of the nurses' list of least favorite patients. I also left with severe short and long-term memory loss and limited muscle control on the left side which caused me to walk with a limp. Still, the only thing that mattered was that I was home, and that I recognized my children and surroundings. I knew I would recover.

Ted had no understanding of the severity of my condition or the frustration that accompanied it. My bones ached, and I was weary with a heaviness that made me feel incredibly old. One night when the kids were in bed, I decided to relax in a hot bath and go to bed early. Sleep seemed like a wonderful idea.

"I need to go drink supper," I said as I excused myself to get ready for bed. Sensing I had used the wrong words, I struggled to remember what had escaped my mouth just seconds before.

"That's not what I meant to say. I wanted to say ... " I became frustrated trying to convey my intention to go take a bath. I stood in the doorway visualizing the tub filled with water, but no descriptive words would form in my head. Ted stared at me, waiting for me to get my act together.

"You're losing your mind," he finally said.

I softly but systematically pounded the door frame with my fist, willing my brain to work. Would I never again be able to communicate? Words I had known all my life eluded me, and I felt empty and isolated.

"Nevermind," I mumbled as I escaped to the privacy of my bath. I knew I was not losing my mind entirely. There was just so much confusion. The part of my brain that dispensed vocabulary was jumbled and I couldn't make heads or tails of it. The harder I tried to concentrate on what I wanted to say, the more I lost my train of thought. I became uncommunicative and limited my interaction with people to polite, necessary phrases.

What happened to all the beautiful poetry I once knew from memory? I loved the English language. Famous quotes or bits of poetry used to roam freely in my head. Now I couldn't remember the word for bathtub! Nowadays when I pointed to a common household item and asked my nearly two-year-old daughter, "What's this?" it was because I needed to know.

Tomorrow will be better, I consoled myself. And it was. Day by day, little by little, remembering became easier. I realized, though, that I was slurring my words. I concentrated on each word when I spoke and counted each victory a major accomplishment.

Every morning, frightened and confused, I allowed the rising sun to drag me into another day simply because I had no choice. The fear of going insane dominated my existence. I couldn't recall anything from childhood except the knowledge that incest permeated it. Meningitis temporarily wiped out my memory of early years and a good portion of recent times. Each night I lay in bed after everyone went to sleep and peace settled over me like a quiet mist reassuring me that I was strong enough and sane enough to survive in this world.

Months later, as I sorted through loose pictures, I came across a photograph of several friends rafting down a river. I didn't remember ever seeing that picture before, and I was horrified to realize one of the people in the raft was Angela.

When had Ted taken her white water rafting? Surely he wouldn't have done that without my permission! She couldn't have been more than seven at the time. We fought major battles over Angela participating in risky activities. Ted saw no danger in anything, and I saw danger in everything where she was concerned. I usually had a long talk with myself and relented over her riding rollercoasters and swimming in the ocean, but I would never have allowed her to don a helmet and life jacket and be at the mercy of amateurs in a raging river. I called Ted at work and demanded an explanation. "You were there, Karen," he said. "You watched us from the observation deck."

"No. I don't believe that! I would never have let her go!" Was he messing with my mind or was my mind messing with me? It went on like that for years and some things were never resolved in my memory.

The illness changed me forever. I did suffer a muddled memory, but I experienced a crystal clear awareness of the present that I had never known before. Short of patience now and anxious to understand myself from a more honest perspective, I could no longer overlook things that bothered me or concede to Ted's wishes when they conflicted with my own. Everything and everyone around me was changing, because I was changing. Gone forever was the totally complacent Karen whose only wish was to please others and have everyone like her.

\* \* \* \* \*

The next spring, Ted and I took the girls on a short vacation. We returned from a day in the mountains to the insistent ringing of the telephone. It took me a moment to identify the hysterical voice mixed with tears and broken sobs that belonged to Kelly's brother, Lance. I understood him to say Kelly was in intensive care and wanted me to know. "I'm on my way," I told him. "What happened? How badly is she hurt?" Lance spoke more calmly now as he corrected me, explaining that Kelly was not hurt, but refused to leave the ICU waiting room.

"She ran over Amber, and they don't know if she is going to live."

"Oh, my God," I prayed as I felt my weak leg give way and my brain tried to absorb what he meant. There was no need to ask what happened now. It was irrelevant. I braced myself against the wall and hugged the phone as if that brought me closer to Kelly's side.

"Tell her I'm on my way." However it happened, Kelly had run over one of her day care children with her car, and I knew she would trade places with her if she could. A serious accident like this was every provider's nightmare.

Amber, of all kids! She was the most well behaved of all the children we kept. Kelly was so safety conscious, and Amber minded her so well. "How did it happen?" I wondered over and over again on the thirty minute ride to the hospital. I could not begin to imagine what Kelly was going through, but I knew she would be devastated.

I found her in shock, unable to accept the severity of Amber's injuries. She clung to life with the help of a respirator and many prayers. After hours of surgery, the hospital listed Amber in grave condition. Kelly described the details of the tragedy over and over, trying to make some sense of it. She had planned to leave them with her assistant and another part-time helper while she went to the craft store to pick up some last minute supplies. Three-year-old Amber escaped from the house and the sitters' care and somehow slid under the car undetected by anyone. All the pieces did not fit, and no plausible explanation could be found. Yet, the accident had occurred, and the damage was done.

A week later, the hospital vigil began taking its toll on Kelly. "I'm sending my kids to my brother's house for a while," Kelly said to me one night in the hallway of the hospital where

Amber lay fighting for her life. "I just can't cope with them right now."

"Aren't you going to wait until school's out?" I asked.

"I can't. I'm not being the kind of mother I want to be to them right now, and I've got to get myself together. My sister-in-law is flying here tomorrow for a few days, and she's going to take the kids back to Michigan with her. I haven't told Cierra or Heather yet, so don't say anything to them about it."

Kelly's mind was on a little girl in intensive care and her heart was there with her. While immensely relieved that her own children were healthy and whole, that relief was tainted with guilt that she had involuntarily caused another mother's anguish. There was no need for anyone to jab the finger of blame at Kelly. She had herself driven it into the very middle of her soul and nailed it there, forbidding her spirit to rest and holding every aspect of her life at bay.

Cierra was delighted to skip the last week of school and, as always, both girls couldn't wait to go to their aunt and uncle's home. When Kelly's workdays ended she could be found in the waiting room outside Amber's unit praying for her and willing her to recover.

"Dear God," she prayed with the fervent remorse of one who deeply regrets a deed she cannot undo, "please heal Amber. If you have to take someone, take me and let her live. She's just a baby."

Months later, Amber's doctors transferred her from the intensive care unit to a private room. Miraculously, she did recover completely, but the experience drained us all. Though we could not know it then, Amber's accident would return to haunt us at a later date.

# Chapter Fourteen

### * * *

I reminded Ted about the incest in my life, blaming that (and rightly so) for my current confusion and unhappiness. It was not anything he did or did not do. It was something internal that I did not understand, and I grew more miserable with each passing day. I loved my children, but found it increasingly difficult to relate to them. Angela seemed bent on making my life a living hell. My gifted child with exceptional intelligence no longer made passing grades in school and seemed to be trying to set a new daily record for being rude and obnoxious to every member of the family. Ted told me about a free incest survivors group he read about in the newspaper. He thought I could fix myself and then fix the family. He implied that our family problems were my responsibility, if not my fault.

I dialed the number and made the arrangements to join a group of six women that would meet once a week. I could hardly wait for it to start. I had lots of questions, and I hoped they had some answers. I could not formulate a concept of what counseling was, but at that point I figured I had nothing left to lose.

The things I wanted most to give my children; security, a good self-image, love, were the hardest things to give. I thought they would and should come easy and naturally. Instead I saw my family falling apart, and I wasn't even sure it was right to try and hold us together anymore. I knew if I were not happy, no one would be happy, and I was miserable. I tried holding on to my religious beliefs, but they didn't produce the results I wanted. I viewed myself as caring about Ted although I never loved him. The loveless marriage produced a lot of stress, and I just was not that strong anymore. My commitment to marriage paled in comparison to what it used to be. I did not want to hurt Ted, but the pressure continued to become more than I could bear. I thought we had once been good friends, but maybe we weren't even that. Maybe we just needed each other. Perhaps we had helped each other grow, but we were not filling each other's needs anymore. I really did not need a partner in my life. Far too independent for that, I simply wanted to be left alone.

Several years earlier, I wanted to go to counseling, but Ted had not been willing. Now he was willing, and I did not even care enough for that. I just wanted out. Our lives each revolved around the girls but not around each other. What love I had left was being used up and not replenished. We were marking time, but not building a marriage. I felt like a cold and lifeless statue being chipped away continuously over the years. I was scarred beyond repair with lost and broken pieces that no one cared to find or replace.

I gave considerable thought to my father during those days. I wondered if he knew the depth of devastation he was causing. Would he have cared? Was he crazy or just evil? I concluded he must have been evil, as I had always thought. Everyone believed I was the apple of his eye, so loved and protected by him. That is what hurt the most, being so misunderstood and not being able to tell the truth, wondering if I would be believed if I did. If he had ever shown remorse or asked my forgiveness, I would have forgiven him. Now it was too late, and there would never be a chance for reconciliation with my father. One thing was certain - throughout my lifetime,

I would never finish paying the consequences for his sins.

I also considered the contributions my mother made to my life. As much as I wanted to blame and accuse her, I found it necessary to temper judgment with mercy. What experiences had led her to believe and behave as she did? Did she have terrible secrets locked away that she could never share? I found it hard to believe that my grandmother would have tolerated abusive behavior from my grandfather, but who knows what went on behind closed doors or hidden from her eyes? Did Mamma feel the need to look the other way because she could not acknowledge her own abuse. Granny fiercely protected her grandchildren, but what kind of mother had she been? Grandaddy did drink to excess. Was our lifestyle so familiar to Mamma's own childhood that she joined the many other parents who perpetuate the cycle of abuse from one generation to another because they can not deal with their own pain, much less that of their children? I could only speculate with few facts to guide me.

I found a measure of relief in knowing I didn't have to be judge and jury for my own mother. I desperately needed to find something in her to appreciate, and there were some good things about her. Regardless of the devastating childhood she provided for me, there was no doubt that she had always sought to do what God wanted her to do. We disagreed wholeheartedly in our interpretations of God's will, but I did learn a valuable lesson from her faithfulness.

She had introduced me to God in such a way that left him a force to be reckoned with. I had to find where He fit in my life. My mother was a fear-based woman who viewed God as someone to be constantly appeased or feared. I chose to be a love-based person who believes God has rules for us for our own benefit because He cares about us. That distinction has made all the difference between her perspective on life and mine.

I was accepted into the incest survivors group and began piecing myself back together. In this group I met Carolyn, who became the sister I never had. Either by coincidence or by Providential design, we lived in the same neighborhood.

The support group lasted six months, and then I went into private counseling. I got to know myself for the first time in my life. I decided I was a good person and worth spending time with. I took out my childhood pictures and poured over them looking for a common thread. Two things stood out right away. Mistrust was evident in the non-smiling faces and in the eyes. And in every pose, even those at the age of 12 months, I held the hemline of my dress in an attempt to keep anyone from lifting it. I discovered upon closer scrutiny that I always wore dresses in pictures taken at home (easier access for Daddy and the Old Testament forbade women to wear men's clothing). Those taken at Granny's house showed me wearing shorts or long pants (Granny's idea that I should wear what made me comfortable).

Yes, a picture *is* worth a thousand words. I could have easily written an essay of that length on any picture before me. In every snapshot of me with my brothers, our roles were evident. I either held the baby or wrapped my arm protectively around a younger brother's shoulder. Randy was always grinning and clowning around. Jeff looked lost, simply there because he had no choice. Micah looked obnoxious, as the scapegoat usually is. Someone could have taught an Adult Children of Alcoholics seminar based on those pictures.

When I began to see how I had filled the caretaker role in my family of origin, I understood why leaving Ted was so difficult for me. How could I abandon him when he was so weak and helpless? How would he manage without me? My counselor helped me realize how heavily codependency ruled my life. My desperate need to be needed outweighed my desire to take care of myself. Eventually I came to realize that Ted could take care of himself if he chose to.

Amidst much heartbreak and tears, Ted finally agreed to move out a few months after I asked him to. He loved the girls, and the break was hard for everyone. To make matters worse, Grandpa Mick had been diagnosed with cancer, and his prognosis was not very hopeful. We still continued to visit with Ruby and Mick and the Joneses at least once a week. Mr. Jones had died several years previously, but Mrs. Jones still cared for Janet at home. Janet could still walk, with help, though totally blind. They both looked forward to our weekly visits.

My counselor said a divorce would free me to be happy and pursue a new beginning for myself. I wasn't ready to handle that much responsibility or freedom yet after twenty years of marriage, so I simply did not take any legal action. I reasoned that I was as good as divorced, because in my heart and mind I had never been married. The benefits of getting a divorce were not real to me. Ted lived in a separate place, and I had many friends and activities to keep me busy. I did sometimes wonder if settling things between us would make life easier for the kids. Still, a divorce cost money, and I did not need one to keep my emotional life intact. Or so I thought.

## Chapter Fifteen

### * * *

"Mom, I think Kevin pooped again!" Maria called from the toy room.

"Be right there," I answered. "Why does he always do this when I'm in the middle of something?" I mumbled to myself. Getting lunch on the table was of utmost importance today. I had to have all the children asleep by 1:00 p.m. Of necessity, I had started a second job, doing alterations for bridal shops. The customers came to my house in the evenings. I had made an exception to my own rule and scheduled a sewing customer to come for a day time appointment today.

"Mom!"

"O.K. Maria, I'm coming."

"He stinks," she complained at the top of her voice.

"I'm sure you'll survive."

I washed my hands, thinking once again how old and dry they looked. I would have to wash them again after I changed Kevin's diaper. The phone rang, disturbing my thoughts. That would be Ginger Galloway calling. Every morning, just like clockwork. Ginger, my fellow day care provider, my link to sanity.

"Hello."

"I hate kids," came a soulful lament. Sometimes Ginger said "good morning" but you could never be quite sure what she would say.

"I do too. I sure am glad I don't have to babysit for a living," I joked. "By the way, they've changed our child care meeting to Wednesday night of next week. Do you want to ride with me?"

"Yeah. Let's go to eat afterwards. Do you know I'm losing two kids?"

"I have two I'd like to lose," I answered as I fished two wayward crawlers out of the pantry and put them back into the toy room. "There's got to be an easier way to make a living."

"There is," Ginger answered, "but it's immoral and illegal and you can catch all kinds of diseases doing it."

"Yeah, but you only have to work a few hours a night, you can stay in bed while you're working, and it pays good," I reasoned.

"It pays some people good. You and I would probably starve to death. Besides, you'd rather be wiping snotty noses and you know it." She was right. Young children were my joy in life. On the other hand, sex was something I had a real problem with. I knew it was supposed to be a special gift God gave men and women to share with each other when they joined their lives in marriage. I liked to imagine it to be wonderful beyond description, a blending of two hearts, bodies, and minds in a physical and spiritual union. That was my surreal view of sex. In reality, though it was physically satisfying, I found the emotional connection  nonexistent at times and disappointing at best.

"Where do you want me to put this?" Maria stood before me holding a very smelly, very dirty diaper all neatly folded and ready to pitch into the trash.

"Ginger, let me call you back. Things just got busy." As I hung up the phone, guilt flooded me once more. I bent to hug my five-year-old who still stood holding the offensive diaper with one hand and her nose with the other.

"Maria, did you change that all by yourself? I'm so proud

of you! And I'm really sorry, honey. I got busy and forgot you told me Kevin was dirty."

"That's okay. But I had to use five wipes. Is that okay?"

Maria was the most self-sufficient child I had ever seen. I was immensely proud of her, but seeing such maturity and self-discipline in one so young pained me. Moments like this when she took over doing my job made me feel like such a failure in the one area in which I really wanted to succeed. Motherhood was all I had ever wanted from life. Since preschool age, I had dreamed of a baby of my own. I had been blessed with two. Looking at Maria now reminded me of just how blessed I was. What did I ever do to deserve her? I must have done something good in my jumbled, miserable past because there she was, standing before me like a tiny angel with an attitude.

Six little faces interrupted my reverie as they gathered around us waiting for me to say, "Let's eat." I felt like the old woman who lived in a shoe. I always felt like that, but that day I firmly believed someone was tightening the shoelaces.

"Line up, gang. Get a hug before you eat." A big believer in hug therapy, I knew I needed it more than the children. They scrambled to their places and immediately began to argue over which blessing to say. At my suggestion, they all joined in the only one we sang together.

"Oh, the Lord's been good to me
And so I thank the Lord
For giving me the things I need.
The sun, the rain, and the appleseed.
The Lord's been good to me."

I sat down with the children and talked to them while they ate, trying to shake a feeling of depression that continued to build as the day wore on. After all, I reasoned, their parents didn't pay me to have a nervous breakdown. I would have to do that on my own time. My own time... an illusive dream. Even

171

bath time for me was not uninterrupted. I learned to move the phone into the bathroom, so I wouldn't have to go as far to answer it just as I settled into my bath.

I kissed Maria on the top of her head and whispered "I love you" in her ear. I remembered being five. I couldn't help but compare myself to her. Maria was so down to earth, so pragmatic. She was too busy exploring every aspect of her real world to have any time for daydreaming. She believed she could do anything and was not easily dissuaded.

My childhood memory of wanting my own orphanage made me chuckle as I surveyed the semi-chaotic scene in my kitchen. Operating a day-care home was not exactly running an orphanage, but it had its similarities.

During one ordinary work day, I bent to tie a four-year-old boy's shoe as we were preparing to go outside for playtime. Suddenly, I recalled a memory so powerful I could only detach myself from the task at hand and watch as though from a distance as the scene from the past played out in my mind. The child before me was no longer that child, but my youngest brother at the same age. I was around ten years old and hurriedly tying his shoe in an effort to get us out the back door before my father could come through the front door. The panic and urgency from that moment in time came rushing back.

Confusion in the toy room brought me back to the present.

"Miss Karen, I can't button my sweater."

"Miss Karen, Lauren's shoe came off."

"Miss Karen, we want to go outside."

One by one, I attended to the children's needs and sent them out the door to play. I retrieved the portable phone from its cradle, settled onto the patio to keep an eye on the children, and called Carolyn.

"The strangest thing just happened. I think I'm going crazy." I related the events to my friend and, as always, she reassured me.

"Oh, I've done that. And it's okay. It passes. Remember when Beth told us about flashbacks in one of our group meetings?"

"No. I don't remember that one!"

"Well, that's because you couldn't relate to it when we were discussing it. Now you can. You just sort of go into a trance while your mind carries you back to relive something."

"It's scary."

"I know. Talk to Beth about it."

At my next private session with my therapist, I did discuss the incident.

"We call that a flashback, and it's very, very normal for that to happen at this point. You are not going crazy; you're recovering." She went on to say, "But, I'm glad you're here. It can be a scary thing and it's even more frightening when you go through it alone without understanding what's happening. It means your mind is beginning to let in little pieces of your past. Let's deal with it one little piece at a time."

"Well, I'm thinking maybe I shouldn't be in counseling right now. I can't quit my job, and I can't afford to space out like that. What if I really get psychotic and something happens to the children while my mind takes these little vacations?"

"Karen," Beth said. "I know you pretty well by now, and I would be the first one to be concerned if I thought you couldn't handle those children or your own children. Believe me, this is a normal occurrence, and you are one step closer to being where you want to be."

So many events were occurring simultaneously in my life, I could not adequately concentrate on any of them. It disturbed me greatly that something from so long ago in my childhood could not be simply forgotten or at least put aside at this time so I could handle more urgent matters at hand. When I slept at night, I was awakened by nightmares so real I could not shake them from my mind for hours. During my waking hours I spent a lot of time reassuring myself that I no longer lived under any man's domination. I read calming, uplifting poetry before I went to sleep. I prayed and most always went to bed with a peaceful attitude. But despite my best efforts to prevent them, the nightmares returned.

* * * * *

Kelly developed several sores that enlarged and refused to heal. I worried with her while she waited two weeks for an appointment with a doctor. He scheduled Kelly for tests that eventually showed advanced stages of diabetes. Over the next year and a half she developed more and more complications, including kidney failure, and she spent more and more time in the hospital. Finally, the doctor told her to get her affairs in order and to prepare for the possibility of losing the battle with the disease.

Kelly can't be dying! I told myself. How can you die from diabetes when you didn't know you had it two years before?

"I just keep remembering that I told God to take me instead of Amber," she said.

"I don't believe God makes deals like that," I said sternly. "You have to re-program your thinking. You are going to live," I assured her. Much too soon though, the time came for me to return the favors Kelly had done for me while I recovered from meningitis. I cared for her two children as she had cared for mine. They slept at our house when necessary, and I drove them to their various schools and activities when she was too sick to do so.

Mick was dying. So was Kelly. My marriage was headed for divorce court. My oldest child was emotionally distraught to the point that she could not function normally, and I was headed for financial disaster even working two jobs. Yet, without a doubt, incest affected me more than all the other events combined. I found myself battling for my own life, too;

fighting anorexia when I didn't want to fight it. I wanted to die, but I knew I had to live.

More and more, my sleep position gave testimony to the internal turmoil. I had always slept in a fetal position with one hand over my mouth and one hand over my vagina. Now I slept even more curled within myself and covered so tightly my vulnerable parts that I often woke myself with pain in my hands or mouth or vaginal area. Counseling brought all the pain to the surface, but it also brought comfort. Now I knew that the sleep position emerged as a subconscious defense mechanism to protect my body. No longer did I awaken with a sickening feeling of shame, wondering if I were a disgusting person trying to masturbate in my sleep.

Facing the abuse I had lived with as a child brought up many issues. Those that were not adequately dealt with in the daytime vied for attention in my sleep. Carolyn, my friend from the counseling group, became my lifeline. I knew I could call on her any time, and she never failed to offer insight and helpful suggestions. Likewise, she shared her most intimate thoughts with me, and she valued my comments.

During one such interchange, we attempted to solicit some divine renunciation of incest. Together we explored the 18th chapter of Leviticus where sexual relations are specifically forbidden with every close relative - except daughters and sons.

My early childhood belief that God created all females for His own sexual pleasure crept back into my being, poisoning my mind against God's character. Why did God not forbid sexual relations with daughters? He forbade it with mothers, stepmothers, aunts, sisters, half-sisters, step-sisters, nieces, daughters-in-law, sisters-in-law, even animals. Are we lower than animals? Are daughters so meaningless to God that we were not even worth mentioning? Perhaps we were, after all, created as our father's property and for his pleasure. This exclusion from God's circle of protection hit me hard, cracking my spiritual foundation.

Carolyn suggested a different theory for our consideration. Since God precluded this list of unlawful sexual relations with the admonition that "No one is to approach any close relative to have sexual relations" maybe that included daughters by presupposition. After all, daughters are the closest close relative a man can have of the female gender. Perhaps God found it unnecessary to state the obvious. For this same reason, the Scriptures do not tell us to love our children. It instructs us to love God, others, our fellowman, strangers, even our enemies. But there is no commandment to love our children. Why? Because our Maker created us in such a way that we instinctively love and protect our offspring. Just as God did not find it necessary to remind us to breathe in order to live, He gave us the instinct to love those we give life to and to refrain from sexual relations with our children, because the very thought is unspeakable. I chose to believe this theory.

The more I delved into the black waters of my incestuous past, the more often a haunting, recurring dream jolted me from my sleep. In it, I stood on a riverboat, just a very small child surrounded by many people. I looked through the railing and saw a little girl just under the age of two drowning in the water. Too shy to tell a stranger, I ran to find my father and begged him to help her. He told me it was not important and to keep quiet about it. This dream had haunted me for thirty years, and it was just as upsetting each time as it had been the first time.

Maybe it represented the child in me dying and my lack of control to do anything about it. All the elements from my life were certainly in the dream: keep the secret, don't tell, lots of people standing around oblivious to the obvious. Or had I witnessed my father actually murdering someone? Had the years and a small child's lack of understanding blended different incidents into one crazy dream? Maybe it was simply a form of grief for the infant sister they told me had drowned in the birth canal. It didn't matter. I couldn't do anything about it either way. I tried to fall asleep again, all the time knowing I would have to check my own children before sleep would come. They were both sleeping peacefully. So safe, so protected, so loved. I kissed them lightly and, reassured, fell asleep myself.

Food became increasingly unappetizing to me. Tea and Coke became my companions. They did not nourish my body, but having a glass in my hand and the motion of sipping helped calm my nerves. There was so little time to think, only time to rush from one activity to another. If Kelly was not in the hospital, then Mick was. If my kids were not fighting with each other, they were fighting with Kelly's kids. If Angela was not in trouble at school, then Maria was sick at school. In the evenings, I juggled sewing customers with Maria and Heather's gymnastics lessons and Angela's allergy shots. In the daytime I tried to provide quality childcare for six preschoolers and be available when my dying friends and their families wanted to talk. I put my divorce on the back burner. My divorce was on hold, but confrontations with Ted escalated. So did the run-ins with Angela.

Because Angela and I had bonded immediately and so intensely from the moment I first held her, we had been like an extension of each other. I missed that closeness very much. Only the memory of that relationship kept me from feeling like a complete failure. I hoped that carefully laid foundation would eventually bring us back together.

Both my daughters were gaining too much weight, and I wanted so much to control it. I really worried about Angela. Thirteen is a terrible age to be overweight. Packaging is everything at that age, and she already suffered so much from insecurity. I did not want her self-esteem to drop any lower. Of all the things a mother cannot control in her teenager, weight is at the top of the list. I knew that without question, but still I tried. I quit buying sweets and began cooking more nutritious food. I exercised with her. I offered incentives. I praised her efforts. I encouraged her to ride her bike. Finally, I asked her pediatrician and her counselor to talk to her about the problem. She gained ten pounds. I lost the same amount. Angela dealt with her weight problem by worrying about my weight loss. She told me I was getting too skinny. I bit my tongue to keep from accusing her of being jealous. I couldn't see my problem any more than she could see hers.

Everyone I knew made comments about me losing weight too fast. They were all genuinely showing concern, but I found it an accomplishment to have enough self-control to lose weight. It was one of the few areas in my life I felt I could control. Comments from childhood have a way of staying with you and surfacing when you are least able to deal with it. Any reference to my body wormed its way into the recesses of my brain and hid there waiting to leap out at me whenever self-confidence ran low. I would still hear my brother chanting, "Fatty, fatty, two-by-four, can't get through the bathroom door."

Being two years older but smaller than your sister is a painful predicament for a ten-year-old boy to be in. If I were average, then he must be a runt. If he could call me fat, for one brief, shining moment he felt average. And we so desperately wanted to be average, to blend in, to be normal. I don't think to be happy was ever our goal. The most I ever hoped for was to be ignored.

Growing up, my Dad's only sister never failed to pat my thighs and coo, "You've got such fat little legs." Meant as a compliment, it always angered me as a child. Angered me even more that people expected me to smile and say "thank you." The adult in me realized that being five feet, seven inches tall and weighing 120 pounds is not fat, but the little girl in me still feared not fitting through the bathroom door.

* * * * *

Maria and Heather were singing in the children's choir at church, practicing hard for the 1985 Christmas program. Kelly and I worked together to make matching frilly, white eyelet dresses with red satin sashes for them.

The day finally came for the Christmas cantata. The girls looked so cute in the little white half-robes with royal blue bows. Both of them were six years old and missing their two front teeth. I could not get enough pictures. Kelly missed the first night's performance. I hurt for her and for Heather. I felt sure she would not make it for the second performance either, but the boundless determination of maternal love proved me wrong.

The next night found us all sitting on the same pew and sharing an unsurpassed spiritual experience. All, that is, except Ted. He had gone the night before, and he had other plans for tonight. I wished he were there, if for no other reason than old time's sake. I knew it would be the last time we would have the opportunity to be together.

Kelly and her brother, Lance, cried a lot. One of the soloists sang "People Need the Lord" and our choir director outdid herself singing "The Light of a Million Mornings." The words of the songs spread it all out before us to be faced together. One of us was dying, and we were all hurting, but heaven was waiting and hope was in our hearts.

I felt bonded to every being in that sanctuary, even the ones I didn't know. Underneath were the everlasting arms upholding me in my time of deepest despair. The congregation was my family, and what a family it was! The service ended with every person in the church holding a lighted candle and singing "everlasting light, everlasting light, shine through the darkness with everlasting light". It was beautiful and moving ... and I was glad when it ended.

We went to Baskin Robbins, honoring our long-time tradition of taking the kids for ice cream treats after they performed at anything. I sat in the car with Kelly, and we talked. She waited until everyone else went inside the building before she turned to me and said, "I thought I was dying last night."

"Tell me what happened. Were you in pain or did you just have a feeling it was time?"

"I woke up choking on my own saliva. I couldn't spit it up, and I couldn't swallow fast enough. I woke Tom and we cried. I prayed I wouldn't suffocate."

I prayed she wouldn't, too. Wasn't it bad enough to have to die at thirty-two? We had a very special few minutes together before we were rejoined by our families. She told me she was ready to die, but she wished she didn't have to. We talked about her fears, and I told her I would watch over her children and help Tom all I could.

Soon afterwards, Kelly went back into the hospital for nerve-block procedures to help control the pain. I welcomed her children back into our household so Tom could spend as much as time with Kelly as possible.

One night, long after the children were in bed, I allowed my pent up emotions to spill. In desperation I cried out to God, "Where are you? And where have you been all my life? If you are so loving and it hurts you to see your children hurt, just where the hell were you when I was a little girl and I needed someone to help me? Where are you now when Kelly needs you?" Too angry to do anything but cry, too confused to listen or understand if Christ himself had appeared before me and tried to explain, I spent the next few hours cursing God and venting my frustration any way that happened to strike my fancy as I attempted to clean house and do the laundry.

A glance at the clock told me it was almost 2:00 a.m. and unfinished chores threatened to eat up the rest of the night. After the last load dried, I looked around at the piles of clean clothes that still had to be sorted and put away. I felt so tired

I collapsed into the mountains of socks and underwear that belonged to five different people. Totally spent, I cried some more and begged God to forgive me for my attitude and to assure me of His presence. I needed to know that He does suffer with us, and that He is with us even when we don't feel His presence.

I was ready now to try to listen to Him. I opened my Living Bible and once again my eyes fell on exactly the message God had for me. In Isaiah 59:15b I read, "The Lord saw all the evil and was displeased to find no steps taken against sin. He saw no one was helping you, and wondered that no one intervened. Therefore he himself stepped in to save you through his mighty power and justice."

Finally! After so many years I had an answer to my most nagging question. I still don't understand how neighbors, doctors, relatives, pastors, school teachers, and social workers could suspect abuse and mind their own business. I do know some possible reasons for their human behavior, and I can accept those. What I could not accept was God not intervening. Now I saw that although God's power is not limited, he is dependent on people to physically reach out and touch a child in need of protection.

I thought of my salvation experience at the age of nine, and I realized what an incredible occurrence that was. God had truly intervened. He came to me where I was, because I was unable to come to Him. That He took a child who dared not trust and brought me into a personal relationship with Him is still a miracle beyond my comprehension.

I could see clearly now that when no one else helped, God told me in my spirit to get out of the house at the age of ten. He protected me and guided me in the right paths. The nights I spent in an open field under the stars were not times of danger for me. God lingered alongside me, protecting me from snakes, and men, and the elements. He guided me away from the temptation of drugs and easy money. Instead, he gave me the determination to finish high school and the desire to go to college. He sent good people into my life to counteract the erroneous examples that were there. I looked around at my four-bedroom house. I thought of my children and my friends, and I knew He was still blessing me.

I had lived a tragic past, and some of it resulted from my own actions. When I surveyed the tracks of my tears, it seemed incredulous that I, the sweet, good child who grew into a loving, dedicated Christian with extremely high morals and good intentions had, in reality, almost ended my own life, cheated on my husband, had an abortion, and would soon be divorced. I realized that all those things were a natural result of my dysfunctional childhood, and without counseling I would have continued on a self-destructive path. There were many things in my past that brought me shame, but I knew God had forgiven me. Most importantly, I had forgiven myself. I chose to applaud myself for those accomplishments that deserved a measure of pride.

No one would ever know how hard I worked to overcome my past or just how much courage it took to face each new day. After years of trying, I could now lift my eyes to speak directly with other people, and I could risk disagreeing when necessary. I had never allowed smoking and drinking to become a part of my life, and I respected myself enough to take care of my body. I could even go for simple medical care when needed without assistance. My other personality had integrated. I no longer needed her to cope for me in any everyday situation.

Most importantly, I had broken the cycle of child abuse and learned better parenting skills than the ones my parents modeled for me. I would never be rich or famous or anyone's hero, but I considered myself successful.

Healing came through many avenues, from the initial

incest survivors' group and the friendships formed therein to individual counseling and other support groups. As my beloved grandmother once said, "Not all learnin' takes place in the schoolhouse." It can also be said that not all healing takes place in psychotherapy. Every person who ever touched my life in a kind and positive way contributed to my healing, but it was I who finally had to demand what I needed for emotional recovery.

I replaced those one-way friendships that took all I would offer and gave nothing in return with healthier friendships with stronger people who enjoyed me for *me*, not for what I could do for them.

I made a light-hearted, but firm announcement to my children that I needed time to myself at night. "If your pants are not on fire or you haven't lost a pint of blood, don't disturb me when I'm taking my bath," I told them. After several false alarms and reminding them of the little boy who cried wolf, they finally got the message. Since my budget was so strained, there was precious little I could do to indulge myself, but I made the most of bath time. Bubble bath and bath oils were something I could afford, so I let the water caress my body each night as I luxuriated in the progress I had made over my life span.

Once, taking a shower or bath had been a torturous ordeal, but time and determination changed all that. Water had become my friend. Once a year, I treated myself to the same ocean that had played Russian roulette with my emotions in my teen years, one day holding me in a grip of terror, the next, soothing my jangled nerves with its rhythmic sound. Mexico Beach became my quiet place, my sanctuary where I could be alone. I still respected the mighty power of the sea and the danger of venturing too far from shore, but I no longer feared the playful edge with white-capped waves crashing against my legs or calm ripples slapping me as if to say hello.

Journalizing anchored me to reality. When thoughts appear on paper, they become more real, more tangible, and more manageable. Maturity, wisdom, and healing came through writing my life's story. I could sort through my confusion and pain, pride and accomplishments, in a very private and beneficial way.

## Chapter Sixteen
### * * *

Carolyn and I had to make appointments to visit with each other since both our houses were bustling with activity and we preferred uninterrupted quality time to more superficial visits. She and I were both changing so much it was hard to keep up with ourselves and each other. We had forged so strong a bond that it surpassed friendship and entered the realm of sisterhood. We understood what the other one felt without exchanging words.

We marveled that we could be so close when, aside from incest, we had nothing in common. We were miles apart in activities and interests. While I attended to my babies all day, Carolyn worked in the local Civil War museum. Carolyn is a music major who loves anything to do with history and avoids small children like the plague. I couldn't carry a tune in a bucket, or remember what happened in my own life yesterday, much less what happened years ago in the world at large.

It was not the amount of time we spent together that made us close, but the knowledge that we would make time for each other on a moment's notice. We based our friendship on talking and listening and caring. There was no condemnation, judging, manipulating, taking advantage of, or criticizing between us. We depended on each other to be honest without being intrusive, to care without being judgmental, to be available without making a nuisance of ourselves, and to love each other unconditionally because no one else ever had.

Scarcely had she sat down for one of our visits when I noticed an angry red mark streaking a good four inches along her thigh.

"What happened to your leg?" I exclaimed.

"I did that," she said matter-of-factly.

"How?"

"I took a pin and scratched it." Again in the same matter-of-fact tone.

"Why?"

"I don't know. I was mad at Paul, and I just did it." She didn't offer any further explanation for the self-mutilation, but we both knew it stemmed from anger turned inward upon herself.

I knew it was going to be a long visit, and I settled back to enjoy it. Our times of getting together were getting fewer and farther between. We sat cross-legged on the bed like teenagers catching up on the news since we last saw each other. She had separated from her husband, but after almost a year decided to try to live with him again.

"Why?" I needed an explanation. I hated her moving back home because I feared the effects it would have on her. Like myself, she spent a lot of time sorting through her past and trying to decide her future. I watched Carolyn in her pain, and I wanted to ease her suffering. She was following closely on my heels, and since I had so recently been in the same situation with Ted, I felt her pain with Paul. She explained she intended to live out her own life right under her husband's nose and torment him with reality rather than changing herself for him.

"What about the guy you met that you said was so easy to talk to?"

"I still talk to him. I've decided to copy you and see how many years I can juggle two men," she teased.

"I don't recommend it. Your attitude sounds good,

though. You know, we really are beginning to take better care of ourselves."

"Yeah, right!" Carolyn laughed spontaneously as she looked at the long scratches on her leg. She flipped her cigarette and rolled her eyes to emphasize her point.

"... said the two anorexics," I added, lifting my glass of ice water and giving it a meaningful glance. My laughter mingled with hers as we became caught up in the absurdity of my remark. I loved Carolyn because we could be women in crises together one moment and giggling school girls the next. She was the one person with whom I could share anything.

"Speaking of taking better care of ourselves, did you ever make an appointment to see about that lump in your breast?" Carolyn asked.

"What do you think?" I answered.

"You know. It's funny that we feel so differently about doctors. You see them as threatening, and I'm just the opposite. I like the attention they give me, and I see them more as friends. Why is that?"

"Because you're crazy and I'm not? I give up. You tell me," I joked.

"You get sarcastic when you're feeling threatened, you know," my friend remarked with a teasing smile on her face.

"Well, I just know that if I needed a friend, I wouldn't look for one in a doctor's office. They never did anything for me."

"That's not true," Carolyn reminded me. They have repaired your bladder several times so you can urinate. They've also helped clear up your poison oak, strep throat, and meningitis. And without that tubal ligation, you would still be worrying about getting pregnant."

"So you're telling me that you have no problem at all going to any doctor of any kind."

"Basically, that's true."

"So, you go for a pap smear once a year, see a doctor whenever you're sick, and have your teeth cleaned every six months like a good girl."

"No! Now, I don't do dentists," she replied far too quickly. "I don't want anyone messing with my mouth."

Hours later, we came to several fascinating conclusions, starting with our commonality of avoiding dentists. Only through close scrutiny of our own unique experiences and through later discussions with our therapist did we come to understand how forced oral sex at an early age made dental care intolerable.

It was not necessarily pain we were avoiding. It was the invasion of our oral cavities by X-ray film, instruments, fingers, and solutions. Certainly flouride treatment does not hurt, but it is, on a subconscious level, a close approximation to semen in the mouth. It can trigger a flashback so repugnant that we gag and panic. Who would have ever associated the two? We would never have tied going to the dentist with incestuous acts, but the correlation for us is undeniable.

Carolyn had far more trouble understanding why getting a chest X-ray presented such a problem for me and for other survivors we knew.

"It's because I have to take my clothes off, and everyone knows I'm naked beneath that hospital gown," I told her. "I feel like I'm being publicly humiliated. When they say, 'Don't breathe', I feel like I'm suffocating. I always have this 'I'm afraid I won't be able to breathe' fear just beneath the surface anyway, and holding my breath for X-rays intensifies that feeling."

"Well, back up a minute to the subject of dentists. When we first met, you had just been to get a crown or filling or something. How were you able to do that?" Carolyn asked.

"Oh, I went around with a toothache until my friend, Ginger, couldn't stand it any longer."

I then told Carolyn how Ginger had called her dentist,

explained the situation, and asked if he would be willing to work with me. As it turned out, an intercessor is exactly what I needed. Her dentist called and asked what I needed to make a visit to his office possible. It felt good to know he cared enough to take even that much extra time with me, and it allowed me to establish a rapport with him before we even met.

We worked out a plan I was comfortable with over the phone which included  having an oral surgeon friend of his meet us at the dentist's office the day after my initial visit. He sedated me while the dentist worked on my teeth.

As Carolyn and I talked about what we each need from doctors, we found we needed different things specifically, but in general we agreed that we feared losing control to an authority figure. While I need them to understand that my psychological dilemma is at least as serious as the physical problem, Carolyn prefers not to divulge her emotional concerns to every doctor she sees. If a medical procedure is a painful one, I *need* to be put to sleep, even if they don't ordinarily do that. I trust the doctors' medical expertice. I just can't endure being violated again.

"Maybe it's the violence and torture from my past moreso than the sexual abuse," I told her. "I don't know. I haven't figured all that out yet."

"Maybe it is," she agreed, "Because it's just the opposite with me. I can't handle being put to sleep. I feel a total loss of control then. The pain doesn't bother me so much, but I need to know what's being done to my body."

Long after Carolyn went home, our conversation replayed in my mind until I began to make some sense of it. Carolyn was right. I owed a measure of gratitude to more than one doctor. I thought back to the two primary physicians who treated  me as I grew up, the gynocologist who treated me as an adult, and the dentist who bent over backwards trying to help me. They were always kind to me and spoke to me with respect and concern. It was my mother who assigned arrogance to them, who made me believe they didn't have time for me and didn't care to hear what I had to say.

There had been good doctors in my life, but there had also been doctors and dentists in my past who saw me only as a troublesome intrusion they would rather not deal with. Perhaps most doctors are too busy to care, but for every arrogant, self-serving doctor there must be one with bedside manners who values his or her patients and will do whatever it takes to preserve a person's life and quality of life.

I decided that for the future I would only see doctors who were willing to talk with me over the phone before I made an appointment. It's important to me to assure them that any other time I am a responsible, mature, productive adult, even though I may behave more like a frightened three-year-old when they see me for the first time. It allows me to maintain a measure of dignity in the midst of divulging my innermost secrets to total strangers. I need them to see me a respectable adult, not just as a pathetic leftover of my father's shame.

\* \* \* \* \*

Angela concentrated on seeing how many ways she could disobey me and still make me love her. I knew that was her game, but I failed miserably in playing my part.

Against my wishes, her father had given her a sun lamp for Christmas a few months back. I did not believe she possessed the maturity to own a sun lamp and I worried that she or the younger children might inadvertently get hurt with it. Sure enough, within three months Angela fell asleep with her face close to the lamp. Already suffering with an ear infection and her ever-present allergies, she had to be rushed to another doctor for the burns. I knew it would be worse the following day.

The first rays of sunshine woke me, and I knew I had overslept. I ran to Angela's room to check on her burns. I stared, horrified, at her oozing blisters and swollen lips. Little slits with red rims replaced the beautiful, sparkling blue eyes that were there just yesterday. This was the worst week so far this year for pollen, and her allergies testified to that fact. She spent most of the day vomiting from the erythromycin the doctor gave her for the infection. I knew she must suffer these results of her disobedience, but I wanted to take away all her pain. I could do nothing except apply the medication the dermatologist prescribed and treat her allergies and ear infection. Only time would diminish the pain and tell how much scarring would remain.

"My beautiful baby," I thought. "Why do you have to learn everything the hard way?" It was her 14th birthday, but it seemed a mockery to wish her a happy one.

That same evening, my new counseling group met for the first time. I hated leaving Angela when she was so sick, but I felt it would be a mistake to cater to her. Besides, I really needed to go. I had learned all I needed to know for now about the incest in my past, but I knew next to nothing about how my father's alcoholism had impacted my life. My quest for knowledge gained speed and volume like a fire raging out of control. The more I learned, the more I had to know. Human nature fascinated me, and I knew absolutely nothing about it. I had always been taught to ignore my human instincts.

At first the new group seemed to be too emotional for me. Even the man in the group cried a lot, but his tears seemed justified to me. He introduced himself as Phil, and he seemed to be sensitive to others and honest with himself. At the end of the session, everyone automatically hugged each other. I was not comfortable hugging strangers, especially since no one warned me about this custom beforehand. After responding in kind to two demonstrative women, I tried to discreetly slip out the door before someone else cornered me. I stopped in the hallway to exchange phone numbers with a woman named

Joan, whom I liked right away. We were having an interesting conversation when the man named Phil walked up to us.

"Are you accepting hugs tonight?" he asked me.

"Yes. And thank you for asking." Ordinarily I would have been very nervous with a lingering embrace. He hugged me close, yet I did not feel threatened. He told me he had never met an incest victim who acknowledged the fact, and he said he admired my candor and my strength. It was the first time a man ever touched me and left me feeling good. He was quite possibly the only man who ever touched me without sexual motivation. Because of that contact that evening, I began to see men in a different light. Could it be that there are some men who have been hurt, admit it, and go on to understand themselves and thus become sensitive and understanding of others? Probably not, I decided, but it was possible. Wasn't it?

# Chapter Seventeen
## * * *

The lawyer suggested I write out what I considered a fair divorce settlement to avoid the extra cost of having the court do that for us. What is fair? How do you measure years of sacrificing self for someone? What is the monetary value of giving up your self-esteem to be a doormat? What compensation will equalize the lost years that cannot be reclaimed? Oh, for an eraser big enough to obliterate all the mistakes of my youth!

There is no value in regrets, but there is power in resolution. There comes a time when blame is no longer important. The anger is spent and we still have the shattered pieces of our lives just waiting for us to do something with them.

I took the shattered pieces of my life, combined it with all the determination I could muster, and prepared for my toughest challenge of all: Learning to trust men.

Late one night, the phone rang. I reached for it, half afraid to answer.

"Hey, this is Phil. Were you sleeping?"

"No. Never!" I replied as I secretly wondered why he was calling at midnight.

As if reading my mind, he said, "I know it's late, but you said this is the most convenient time for you. I hope you were serious about that. Is this too late?"

"No! I won't go to bed for a couple of hours yet. What's wrong?"

"Nothing. I just called to see how you are. I missed our Wednesday night survival class and I thought I'd see how your week is going."

I thought to myself, a man calling to see how I am and not needing anything for himself? This might be interesting.

Aloud, I asked, "How was California?" He told me about his latest business trip and I thought how good the unexpected call made me feel. We talked for another hour and a half.

I was doubly blessed to have Phil in both the counseling group and a divorce support group I attended. I valued his input immeasurably, and I attributed our acquaintance to no less than divine intervention. He had the strong religious convictions that I still had hidden somewhere deep within me. Phil had inner strength and a squeaky clean outward appearance that gave no hint of the pain and frustration he carried. I, on the other hand, had discovered a few curse words not previously in my vocabulary. What's more, I discovered that sometimes it just feels good to say them! Phil never once condemned my language or my behavior. He didn't have to. My conscience convicted me whenever I said anything out of line.

\* \* \* \* \*

Everyone I knew tried to convince me I should change jobs. They all believed that six children all day long five days a week were wrecking my nerves, not to mention my house. I remained just as convinced that those six children were the glue that held me together. They appreciated and loved me, and I didn't feel that from any one else with the exception of Maria and Carolyn.

On one particular day, little Colby, one of the toddlers in my day care, giggled and ran to me with arms outstretched. I picked him up and hugging him close, spun around and around sharing his delight. His infectious laughter spread throughout the room. Soon everyone joined our game of spinning in circles. I kissed Colby's baby nose as we fell into a dizzy heap into the blankets on the floor. One by one the other babies fell on top of us.

I fleetingly thought of Sugar and Honey and the memory of those sweet black ladies caused me to laugh aloud at prejudice and its misconceptions. Now I fully understood integration. Maria's beautiful brown Latin American skin lay next to Daniel's smiling Oriental eyes. Colby's kinky black hair and skin contrasted with blond-headed Blake. Tyler's big blue eyes sparkled in his Caucasian face as he linked arms with Amanda, his brown-eyed, curly haired Jewish counterpart. We looked like a poster for UNICEF and I loved it.

Life is good, I thought, if you choose to see the good in it. I had given up on dying. I was as healthy as a horse. And if I were going to live, I had to do it with purpose. I discovered I really wanted to do so many things. I decided to travel, go to college, write a book, and when the right time came, change professions.

I decided to enjoy every day and to surround myself with people who were good for me. I forced myself to do something just for fun every day, gave myself time-outs when I felt stressed, and set aside some crying time when no one would see.

In early April, Granny Ruby took Grandpa Mick to the hospital for the last time. Angela and Maria were in Florida with their father for spring break. Mick asked repeatedly when the girls were coming home. I promised to bring them to the hospital as soon as they got back to town. When they did return, it was just before midnight. I knew Mick might not make it through the night, and both girls wanted to go see him despite the late hour. We had a short visit, but he was alert and able to hug them and tell them he loved them. Grandpa Mick died within an hour after we left the hospital.

The day of his funeral coincided with the day Carolyn and I planned to leave for a five-day getaway to Florida. I attended the funeral, but decided to skip the burial ceremony. Carolyn met me at the funeral home, and we left from there. In her warm and wonderful way she urged me to share my feelings. I decided, however, that my grief could be put on hold for a few days. This was our time together that we' d planned for so long, and I didn't want to spoil it.

We drove with the top down on her convertible like two schoolgirls and let the wind blow the tension from our bodies. The six-hour trip took almost nine hours because we stopped at my grandmother's house to plunder through the antiques, and for me to share my memories with Carolyn. We took our time on the way down. It was late when we arrived and we welcomed our beds in the condo we had rented.

Morning found me on the beach enjoying the solitude and the sounds of nature. I let Carolyn sleep in until I could stand it no longer. We teased each other about me being the smart one and her having all the beauty.

When Carolyn finally had enough coffee in her to get her going, we embraced the beach and sun and sand with open arms. The deserted shoreline provided a private beach in the middle of civilization. What better place to bare our souls and lift our spirits? We spoke of men and love and life and substitutes for all of those.

Efforts to build sandcastles on the beach were soon abandoned in search of the more elusive sand castles in the air. We spun dreams like cotton candy. We took turns snapping pictures of each other with her instant camera and watching them develop. Fully relaxed in our skimpy swimsuits, it was a scene whose time had come. Our laughter mingled with the call of seagulls and the roar of the ocean waves. We were light-hearted children enjoying precious, rare moments of total freedom.

Darkness provides a safe canopy for dealing with painful issues. Reality is harsh enough without airing it in bright sunlight. All seriousness was postponed by unspoken, mutual consent until late night discussion. Only then were the broken fragments of our lives exchanged once again. We were each other's microscope, examining and probing for new ways to deal with old problems.

I needed those four days of relaxation to help me cope with the days ahead. Life's duplicity threw me joys and sorrows faster than I could process either one.

One balmy evening in May, Kelly called me. "Hi. It's me. Can you go out somewhere tonight? I'm feeling good enough to leave this house, and I've got cabin fever."

I asked her to pick a place, while I found a sitter for my children. Because of Kelly's deteriorating condition, she needed to go somewhere we could leave if necessary without disturbing anyone. She could not sit still for long and had to have a chair she did not have to lean back against because of her kidney drainage tube. A movie was out of the question and that was the only suggestion I could coax from my overworked brain. Kelly suggested I call my friend Sarah and ask her to join us.

"Ask her to figure out where we can go that we would all enjoy," Kelly pleaded.

We ended up at a popular country and western dance club nearby. I had never been, but I fell in love with the whole atmosphere. All three of us were fascinated with the line dances. The music grew on us as the rhythm of the night caught us in its spell-binding web. Kelly vowed that when they removed her kidney and she recovered enough, she was going to come back and learn every dance. I didn't doubt that at all, but I did have my doubts that Tom would ever learn to two-step with her.

Sarah and I stole discreet glances at a row of apparently

single men standing along the back wall. Kelly joined us in our little game of trying to choose the most appealing one. We finally agreed that one was superior to all the others, at least from that distance in the dark.

We discovered the club offered free dance lessons twice a week. Sarah and I made plans before we left to check it out. After two hours, Kelly's pain medication began to wear off, and we decided to leave and get her home.

If we had left when we first decided to instead of listening to "just one more song", my life would have probably continued along in its mundane way indefinitely. Instead, it was forever changed somewhere in the middle of the next song. So engrossed was I in leaning over the balcony railing and watching the precise, coordinated movements on the dance floor that Sarah had to tap me on the arm to let me know someone was asking me to dance.

Panic overtook me as my eyes traveled upward to see the man of our choice from the line-up leaning slightly on our table and looking with amusement into my face.

"Would you like to dance?" Simply put.

I heard my voice responding just as evenly, "I'd love to, but I don't know how. Thanks for asking, but I'll have to pass."

"It's easy. Come on. I'll show you how."

"No. I'm sorry. I really can't dance with you, but you're both welcome to sit here if you would like to join us."

Thinking I had just given him a polite brush off, I waited for him to excuse himself and find someone else with whom to dance. Wordlessly, he motioned to his friend and they walked away from our table. I exhaled slowly, shaky with relief. To my surprise, they returned almost immediately, bringing two chairs with them.

"What do I do now?" I muttered into Sarah's ear as we made room for them at our table.

"Get to know him," she replied calmly.

Later, I had no idea what we said. I concentrated on keeping my knees from knocking by locking my ankles behind the front legs of the chair. When Kelly indicated she had to leave, he asked for my phone number. I countered by asking for his and promising to call.

In the privacy of my car, Sarah extolled his good looks, remarking about the thick gold chain around his neck, how his shirt was tastefully unbuttoned just two buttons. Very sexy, not tacky. Three would have been too many. With that gorgeous tan he must work outside a lot. And did I notice how well groomed he was? How neatly clipped his mustache was?

I had to admit that my fear and nervousness caused none of that to register. I only knew that there was a male presence beside me, and that I was trying to not say anything stupid.

"You are either handing us a lot of bull, or you covered yourself very well. No one could have told you were nervous." Sarah was, once again, making me feel better about myself.

"I'm telling you, Karen, he is very, very good looking. And he is interested in you. You should call him this week before too much time goes by."

"Call him," Kelly instructed when I looked in her direction.

McCall was only in my life a few months, but he brought color to my world, and touched in me emotions I never knew were there. He was a stepping-stone, a necessary notch in my understanding of men, and in my ability to relate to them.

There were other men in my life after McCall, and one of them was intuitive enough to realize that I was self-conscious about my body. Chad helped me learn to appreciate my body and see myself in a way I never had before.

"I find this impossible to believe, but you really don't see yourself as desirable to men, do you?" he said to me one evening as I was destroying an intimate moment.

"Not really."

"Karen, you are intelligent and funny and I know twenty-year-olds that would kill to have a body like yours. Take a long look in the mirror sometime and tell me just what it is you would change if you could. If you are honest with yourself, I think you will like what you see."

That very night, I dared to accept Chad's challenge. I took advantage of the opportunity of being alone for the night. After my bath, I stood naked before my daughter's full length mirror and scrutinized myself from head to toe.

I grudgingly admitted that my physical body could be in worse shape. What really bothered me was the difficulty I encountered just looking in the mirror. I heard the authoritarian voice of my mother preaching against vanity, warning of the hell prepared for harlots.

The real challenge came when I tried to look myself in the eye. I covered my body with a towel so I could confront myself face to face. Initially, quick, passing glances were all I could manage. Eventually I was able to scan the nude image before me, allowing my eyes to rest on one area, then another, facing the hot flames of shame and knowing this time I could not run away.

Finally, I forced myself to stare into the eyes of the reflection before me. The dull, vacant gaze of sadness stared back. Suddenly, the years fell away, and the eyes so full of pain and confusion rained quiet tears as I forced myself to watch. The thirty-five-year-old face looked into the mirror and saw a seven-year-old looking back. A tender, loving child had lost a part of her soul to forces she could not understand.

"Your mother was wrong," the woman told the child. "And your father was wrong. But you are a good girl. You deserved better parents. They lied to you about so many things. There's nothing wrong with looking in the mirror. You are lovable and you are desirable, but you can choose who you give your body to. It doesn't belong to every man that wants it.

It didn't belong to your father."

I turned away from the mirror and turned out the light. Sitting on the floor, clad only in the towel wrapped securely around me, I folded my arms around my shoulders, and rocked back and forth, hugging the woman and hugging the child, comforting both.

I came to the realization that since a man had caused the most devastation in my life, only a man could restore my confidence in the opposite sex. The men in the counseling groups helped do that. All had been hurt by the women in their lives, and they related to the unfairness of life. I found them sensitive and willing to share their innermost thoughts.

Phil caught up with me in the hallway of the church when the divorce support group ended one night in early September.

"What do you have to eat at your house?" Phil grinned to show he knew he was inviting himself over.

I laughed and said, "I don't know. I'm sure there is something there you can get happy with. Follow me. I'll fix you something." This was getting to be a habit, but I wasn't complaining. I loved our Wednesday night chats.

We met at my house, and over a hastily prepared meal of fried pork chops, broccoli, and canned corn we shared the latest details of his divorce proceedings and my newly acquired independence. Having Phil for a friend was wonderful. We could share our lives completely and without fear of how the other would feel about it. The totally platonic relationship gave us ease to be ourselves with each other. I depended on Phil for a male's perspective on dating matters. Likewise, I provided some female insight to him when he asked.

"So. How are you doing?" he asked as he settled onto the sofa with a cup of coffee in hand.

"I'm fine. Anything fun going on in your life this week?" I answered.

"That concerns me," he said. His tone commanded my full

attention.

"What concerns you? That I'm doing fine?" I gave him a small smile as I sat across from him on the other sofa.

"It concerns me that you always say you're fine. People say they're "fine" when they really mean something else, but they don't want to talk about it. So, I wonder how you really are, especially since you talked in group tonight about Kelly being worse."

"Yes," I told him. "I got ready to go see her this afternoon, but my sitter cancelled and it was just too much hassle to try to find another one I could trust to handle all eight of the kids. My two are at Ted's for the night. I'll go later on. I can see her anytime."

"Maybe you should go now," he offered. "We can visit some other time."

"No. Thanks. She could linger for weeks like this, and I don't want to cut our visit short. I only see you once a week when we can really talk, and we have lots to talk about."

"Yes, we do," he said, "and one of the things we have to talk about is how you are holding up under all this strain. I don't see you letting your feelings out. I just want you to know you can talk to me, and I think you need to talk to somebody."

I was not being distant with Phil. He created an atmosphere of openness and honesty that allowed me to share my feelings with him. If I were being distant with anyone, it was myself. If I lost my composure, the torrent of grief would overwhelm and crush my status quo, rendering me helpless to cope with everything else in life. I tried to stay in the center of myself, knowing I was walking the tightrope of life without a safety net. I still fought emotional dependency on men while longing for the intimacy we all need.

The phone rang, but I ignored it, not wanting to interrupt our conversation. When the caller tried again two more times and didn't leave a message on the answering machine, Phil suggested I take the call.

"It could be about Kelly," he said.

"It probably is," I said. Then, as realization gripped me, I said again sadly, "I'm sure it is."

I answered it on the next ring.

"Karen. This is Lance." I could sense him trying to get control of his voice, and I waited for him to continue. "Kelly is dead. She died about four o'clock."

"Oh, Lance, I'm so sorry. I was getting ready to come to the hospital soon. Do you want me to come down there or is there something else you need me to do instead?"

"We don't need anything, Karen. There is nothing you can do. She went so easy. She just closed her eyes and quit breathing. She didn't struggle, and she just looked like she went to sleep."

I let him talk until he had nothing more to say. I was almost at a loss for words. I felt a deep sadness, for myself, for Kelly's children, and for mine.

"Lance, you know I'm here for all of you. Whatever you need, just let me know. Take care, and call me tomorrow," I said as we ended the conversation.

I held the receiver that confirmed the news I had just lost my good friend of fourteen years, and I looked into the face of my new friend and saw concern and compassion there. Yes, a door had closed, but an open window beckoned.

\* \* \* \* \*

I missed Kelly terribly and I did not understand why she had to die, but I knew that for me, life would go on. In the months to come, I learned to accept myself for who I am and my life for what it is. I reached a point of celebrating life for better or worse, although so many questions remained unanswered. I knew I could and would surrender the horrors of my past, the pain of my present, and the insecurity of my future to the One who holds all time in His hands.

Not all questions remained unanswered. Occasionally, bits and pieces of information would come to me when least expected. Other important facts were excavated as carefully as diamonds hidden deep beneath the surface of the earth.

Over thirty years passed since the lake incident that left my memory and emotions shattered with only a ball of fear connecting me to that time period. I felt a real need to talk to my cousin, Lisa. We lost touch as teenagers and I wanted to see her again. It took several years to find someone who could locate her for me. It took even longer for Lisa to return my call. Being six years older than me, she had memories I did not have. She felt I would somehow blame her for my pain.

When Lisa finally called me, we talked an hour on a long distance conversation about memories of my father. Strangely, she too, was haunted by something about the lake. What she did clearly remember supplied major pieces in the jigsaw puzzle of my life.

Lisa related chilling details of my father trying to rape her at the lake. When she fought him, he dragged her into the lake and held her under until she ceased struggling. He left her for dead beneath the murky water. I understand from Lisa that I watched helplessly from the bank, frozen in terror. I was six years old at the time. She was barely thirteen.

Because Lisa knew enough to go limp and play dead before all her strength and air were exhausted, she survived the attack. She made her way back to the car in time to hear my father threatening me with words that would silence me until years after his death.

"If you say a word to anybody I'll cut your tongue out!" he hissed at me.

Cold chills raced over the surface of my skin as the enormity of her words settled into my being. I searched through my memory bank, and as recognition began to piece times and events together I thought, Yes! That makes sense!

That's why I quit talking at age seven. That's why I'm terrified of the lake. That partly explains my recurring dream that someone is drowning. That's why I knew something happened to Lisa, even though my consciousness still blocks all memory of the incident!

It was she who told my mother that my father was molesting me. Yes! Yes! Yes! Someone is validating my memories. I'm not crazy! Thank you, Lisa. Thank you for sharing the truth that is helping set me free.

Healing comes slowly, but it does come. Some things a child usually learns at two, three, or four years of age, I did not learn until my twenties, thirties, or forties. Things like trust, confidence, social skills, making choices, having fun... the list goes on and on. I cannot focus on "what if's" and "what might have been's"; only "what is". No matter what was, I have the right and the responsibility to grow from there.

My heart breaks when I remember some of the mistakes I made in raising my children. I have to remind myself constantly that I did the best I could do with what knowledge and ability I had at the time. Hindsight is always 20/20, and I refuse to beat myself up with mistakes of years gone by. I rejoice in the fact that both my daughters have grown into beautiful young ladies who love me in spite of my shortcomings.

At the time of Kelly's death, I had come to understand and appreciate the resiliency of the human spirit. I had not yet found the same appreciation and understanding of the *beauty* of the universe. Only now am I beginning to expect good things from the world around me. It is a constant source of wonder to me that the more I expect, the more I am rewarded. I know we are all responsible for our own happiness, and the more control I gain over my own life, the more I believe that life truly is worth living.

# *EPILOGUE*
### * * *

I wish I could say my past is buried forever. While it no longer controls my life, it will forever affect it. It has taken a lifetime of work to overcome the insidious effects of child abuse. It will require much more painstaking effort of taking one day at a time. I trust the creativity of the child within and the determination of the woman without to make something beautiful of my life.

If it is true that our concept of God is only as good as our relationship with our earthly father, then it is a miracle I desire any relationship with God at all. I have rejected my childhood image of God, the image someone else created and handed down to me. Mamma's angry, harsh, punitive Heavenly Father is not one to whom I can relate.

My God laughs and enjoys his children. He forgives and praises and loves with a pure and wholesome love. He is strong, and he is tender. He cares, and he is present with us at all times. He cares about all of his creation. Because he loves us, he gives us freedom of choice to worship him in whatever way we choose or not to worship him at all. I'm secure in my relationship with my Heavenly Father, and I'm always willing to share my spiritual thoughts, but I reject the notion that I must convince others to believe as I do. I gave up that codependent attribute when I realized the spirit of God will speak to every soul on this earth and how they respond to their understanding of a Higher Power is totally up to them. Releasing myself of that responsibility allows me to enjoy and appreciate my friends from different religious persuasions without trying to change them.

Do I forgive my parents? That depends on one's definition of forgiveness. I carry no grudges, refusing to let my hurt turn into hatred. My energy is directed toward turning my fears into faith and action. I do not wish either of my parents ill, either in this life or the next. I do, however, place the responsibility squarely on their shoulders for their misconduct and the resulting damage they inflicted on my brothers and me. I believe my parents will have to give an account to God for the way they lived their lives, and I am content to leave them in his hands.

To those who choose not to look too deeply, it would appear that Randy and I emerged unscathed from the violent clutches of our childhood. Not surprisingly, the clown of the family, the child who scoffed at danger, went into police work. Randy found a legal and acceptable way to confront the drunks and abusive members of society. He served in all the dangerous areas from street cop, to undercover drug operations to the dive team, trained to recover bodies from black water. Finally, he served as a homicide detective, an area of special interest to him. For a hobby, he chose skydiving. I remain convinced he did that for the sole purpose of upsetting his sister!

Randy married at seventeen and raised three children with no major complications. On the surface, at least, they are a true version of the perfect family. That is what I see, and that is all I want to see. Because Randy suffered the least abuse and because of his personality type, circumstances place him as the most likely to succeed.

We live less than ten miles from each other, but we rarely speak or visit. We have nothing in common, but we know we love each other. We don't hesitate to call if we need a favor, and we never refuse to help each other. I like Randy as a person, and I respect him. I hope and believe the feeling is mutual.

Jeff never found the strength to break away from our mother's domination. Even into his late thirties, he continues to live next door to her, giving her part of his paycheck each week. According to Mamma, he fought a successful battle against drugs and alcohol for many years. He avoids people because he never learned to socialize, and he is uncomfortable when others are around. When we chance to be in the same place at the same time, our eyes rarely meet.

He almost married his high school sweetheart ... three times. Each time, Mamma interfered and Jeff called off the wedding. Finally at the age of thirty, the love of his life married someone else. Jeff still lives alone. He suffers severe back pain. When I see him walking with a limp, I remember Daddy kicking him with his steel-toed work boots. Jeff. He's still my baby brother. When I see him, I see a blond haired four-year-old with sky blue eyes begging me to sleep at home tonight. My throat constricts and my eyes mist over. I am just as uncomfortable meeting his eyes as he is mine.

My oldest brother served in the Marines for a while before choosing a Naval career. It's hard to say where he is in his life now. We have been out of contact with each other for many years. The last time I had a real conversation with Micah, his sympathies lay with Daddy. Perhaps the little boy in him is still seeking his father's approval. Micah seemed to me to suffer from illusions of grandeur and extreme paranoia. He complained of having several fatal diseases, and does indeed seem to suffer physical pain.

Only Mamma knows where he lives. She's the only one he trusts. He is afraid the rest of us are out to get him. Us, and the CIA. Sadly, none of us have the emotional energy to try to convince him otherwise. Mamma says his location has to remain a secret because he has a high position with the Navy. She says he is one of the top men in charge of the security of this country. Mamma believes that. She is the only one who does.

Micah is still her favorite child. He always will be. He is the firstborn son. In her antiquated religious convictions, Micah is the only one qualified to have an opinion, and anything he does is excusable on some level. He has been married three times, but his first two wives proved unfit for him for some reason. Even though divorce is forbidden in my mother's eyes, she could justify Micah's, because he had the misfortune of getting two bad wives.

My life is finally on the right track, one that leaves me congruent with myself. I did take advantage of the free country/western dance lessons (much to my mother's dismay) and found it to be wonderful therapy. As with most abuse victims, my body was stuck, frozen by guilt and a physical inability to move freely. After years of being taught (and believing) that dancing in any form is a sin, it was not easy to integrate it into my life. Before long, however, the invigorating music and choreographed movements brought my body, mind, and spirit together into one complete being.

I won the argument with myself, but was not so successful with my mother. I did not wish to confront my mother, but I needed to put to rest her critical, demoralizing comments every time she found out I went dancing. After one of her "I raised you better than that" mini-sermons, I reminded her that Ecclesiastes says there is a time to dance.

"And my time is Fridays at 7 o'clock," I teased. "Mamma, my moral convictions don't change because I dance, and I don't go dancing because my moral convictions have changed. I dance because I enjoy it. I finally found something I'm good at. How can something that is good exercise and improves my self-esteem and introduces me to new friends be bad?"

I never convinced my mother that I'm a good person, but the good news is I don't have to. When I live up to my own moral standards and am consistent with my own values, there is an inner peace that eliminates the pressure to please everyone else. I didn't feel the need to please her, but I longed for her approval. She's my mother, and a mother is supposed to be proud of her children. Accepting the fact that she will never approve of me is a grief process. It still hurts when I think of it, but I think of it less and less.

Though I have overcome a myriad of problems caused by my childhood, I still suffer from a life threatening phobia of doctors and hospitals. When pain is inflicted upon my body or when my personal space is invaded by medical personnel, my psyche cannot handle the trauma. I fear a second personality returning if I should need emergency medical care. To prevent that possibility, I lead a very cautious life and avoid doctors at all costs. Imagine, all that childhood trauma now transferred into adult agony so neatly packaged under the benign label of "Post-Traumatic Stress Disorder".

Upon reflection of my lifetime of experiences involving medical personel, I realize that I misinterpreted their lack of knowledge of my psychological needs as lack of concern. I expected them to know what I needed when I didn't even know. Now I can analyze and verbalize enough to give them an assessment of the problem and what I need from them, but in an emergency situation, I still need a mommy, someone to intercede on my behalf.

There is enough time and healing between the pain of my past and my life today that it's possible to recall childhood memories without reliving them. But my heart aches with compassion for the countless number of nameless, faceless children who wake up every morning and go to bed every night with the same senseless pain in their lives.

I think of all the three- or five- or twelve-year-olds today who must endure terribly painful procedures to repair damage from child abuse. Thousands of children of all ages too scared to cry, but if you look closely, you can see the fear in their eyes. Too proud to ask if it will hurt or if they have to get undressed, though they may be dying to know. Too defeated in spirit to think they have a right to ask for anything, even information concerning medical procedures which will once again violate their bodies.

And I think of all the patients in medical hospitals and mental health facilities who are confined to their beds by use of restraints. Do their doctors, however well-intentioned, know that they may be trading one problem for another? They may be helping to keep their patients safe physically, but do they have any idea what that does psychologically to the ones who were tied to the bed by their rapist or to the patients whose parents tied them to doorknobs for hours on end?

Are their doctors concerned enough to practice human kindness along with medicine? Will anyone provide them with a cuddly stuffed animal to keep them company in the lonely, frightening hours ahead. Will someone tell them what to expect and hold their hands until it's over?

I would like to see doctors change their new patient forms to include a few questions regarding family and medical history that would ask if the patient was abused or inappropriately touched as a child. If the patient answers "yes", the doctor has a perfect opportunity to ask the patient if he or she has been able to work through the issues surrounding abuse with a professional therapist and if they need any special considerations while receiving medical care.

Many survivors will still feel so much shame and fear of not being believed that they will not even be able to check "yes" on the form, but they will immediately realize they are in the office of someone who cares enough to ask.

People suffering from Post Tramatic Stress Disorder or exhibiting multiple personalities do not respond well to surprises. For those who were tortured as children, many things in an exam can trigger recollections of abuse. Giving them reassurance, a thorough explanation of what to expect, letting them set the pace of the examination or procedure, and allowing them to bring a friend into the room with them are a few things that help most survivors feel more secure. Doctors have a unique opportunity to assist in recovery or add further trauma and inability to trust.

My *dream* is that someday there will be medical doctors who are trained in Post-Traumatic Stress Disorder, and who are willing to work with patients to negotiate the best health care for those afflicted.

My *hope* is that we will all do our part to prevent abuse in any form and that we will lessen the aftermath for survivors by being more understanding and less judgmental of each other.

My *mission* is to be the best that I can be, because I believe when we better ourselves we better those around us.

My *prayer* is that victims will find comfort in the love and caring of others, and that through our mutual support we will all find the world a safer, kinder place.

To those who struggle with the shackles of their past and to their loved ones who live in its shadow, may your courage be rewarded with peace and your lives be blessed with joy.

# About the Author

Karen Austin is zealous in her efforts to break the cycle of child abuse and help others overcome the negative effects of an abusive childhood. She fascilitates divorce recovery and incest survivor groups in her community and gives talks to day care providers and parents on developing better parenting skills.

Ms. Austin attends Kennesaw State University where she is majoring in Public and Social Services.

After spending 25 years in childcare, she retired in 1998 to devote more time to writing and to her family. She enjoys writing inspirational novels and is working on her second book.

Karen Austin lives in the North Georgia mountains.

If you would like to write to Karen Austin
you may do so at the following address.
She would love to hear from you.
Please include a self-addressed, stamped envelope
for a reply.

Karen Austin
c/o Snowbird Books, Inc.
P.O. Box 22
Woodstock, Georgia 30188-0022

# RESOURCES

## VIDEOS

What Do I Say Now?
By Committee For Children
To order: 1 800 634-4449
*Teaches parents how to talk to their children in non-threatening ways about how to protect oneself from abuse

Break the Silence: Kids Against Abuse
By Arnold Shapiro Productions (1994)
Most appropriate for ages 8-15
*Excellent video for explaining different forms of child abuse and how children have coped with and healed from abuse

Hear Their Cries: Religious Responses to Child Abuse
Not in My Church
Not in My Congregation
By Center for the Prevention of Sexual and Domestic Violence (1991)
(206) 634-1903
*Older teens and adults

Identifying, Reporting & Handling Disclosure of Sexually Abused Children
By Committee for Children (1988)
*Target audience: school teachers and personel

Scared Silent: Exposing and Ending Child Abuse
By Arnold Shapiro Productions (1992)
Hosted by Oprah Winfrey
*Older teens and adults

## BOOKS FOR ADULT SURVIVORS

*Incest and Sexuality: A Guide to Understanding and Healing*
by W. Maltz and B. Holdman (1987)
Lexington Books: New York * ISBN 0-669-14085-6

*Secret Survivors: Uncovering Incest and Its Aftereffects in Women* by E. Sue Blume (1990)
John Wiley and Son's Pub. * ISBN 0-471-61843-8

*United We Stand: A Book for People with Multiple Personalities* by Eliana Gil (1990)
Launch Press: Walnut Creek, CA

*Victims No Longer* (for male victims of sexual abuse)
by Mike Lew (1990)
Harper & Row: New York * ISBN 0-06-097300-5, PL

*Women Who Hurt Themselves: A Book of Hope & Understanding* by Dusty Miller (1995)
Basic  ISBN 0-465-09219-5

*Can I Look Now: Recovering from Multiple Personality Disorder* by M. Evers-Szostak and S. Sanders
R. Downing

## FOR PARENT, PARTNERS AND OTHER FAMILY MEMBERS OF SURVIVORS

*Abused Boys: The Neglected Victims of Sexual Abuse*
by M. Hunter (1991) Fawcett * ISBN 0-449-90629-9

*Allies in Healing: When the Person You Love was Sexually Abused As a Child* by Laura Davis (1991)
HarperCollins Publisher: New York * ISBN 0-06-096883-4

*If She is Raped: A Guidebook for Husband, Fathers, and Male Friends* by Alan McEvoy and Jeff Brookings (1991)
Older teen and adult males

*Outgrowing the Pain Together: A Book for Spouses and Partners of Adults Abused As Children*
by Eliana Gil: (1992) New York * ISBN 0-440-50372-8

*When the Bough Breaks: A Helping Guide for Parents of Sexually Abused Children* by Aphrodite Matsakies
New Harbinger Press

## AGENCIES

The Center for the Prevention of Sexual and Domestic Violence
936 North 34th Suite 200
Seattle, WA 98103
(206) 634-1903 Fax: (206) 634-00115
This agency provides information to help the religious community deal with sexual and domestic violence.

The Marilyn Van Derbur Institute, Inc.
P.O. Box 61099
Denver, CO 80206
(303) 322-9374 (fax)
This organization addresses concerns of victims through videos, cassettes, and speaking engagements. It is particularly helpful to those professionals in the medical and mental health field who wish to better serve their patients who are survivors of childhood trauma.

National Committee for Prevention of Child Abuse
332 South Michigan Avenue
Suite 950
Chicago, Illinois 60604 * Phone: 312 327-1500

# Order Form

Please send me _____ copies of
*Blind Trust: A Child's Legacy*
@ 13.95 each (GA residents add 5% sales tax)
20% discount for orders of 10 or more.
ISBN 0-9665191-0-8

(soft cover only)...Total Price          $_____
S&H $4.00 for first book and
$2.00 for each additional book
                        Total S&H          $_____
          Total Amount Enclosed          $_____

Make check or money order payable to: **Snowbird Books, Inc.**
For immediate shipment, mail this form with payment to the
following address:

> Snowbird Books, Inc.
> P.O. Box 22
> Woodstock, GA 30188

Ship to:

_____
Name

_____
Street Address

_____
City

_____
State                        Zip Code

Phone: 770 924-4384 Fax: 770 926-9696
***Thank you for your order.***

# Order Form

Please send me _____ copies of
*Blind Trust: A Child's Legacy*
@ 13.95 each (GA residents add 5% sales tax)
20% discount for orders of 10 or more.
ISBN 0-9665191-0-8

(soft cover only)...Total Price     $_____
S&H $4.00 for first book and
$2.00 for each additional book
                 Total S&H     $_____
    Total Amount Enclosed     $_____

Make check or money order payable to: **Snowbird Books, Inc.**
For immediate shipment, mail this form with payment to the
following address:

         Snowbird Books, Inc.
         P.O. Box 22
         Woodstock, GA 30188

Ship to:

_____
Name

_____
Street Address

_____
City

_____
State             Zip Code

     Phone: 770 924-4384 Fax: 770 926-9696
       ***Thank you for your order.***